The Web of Crime That

SIMON & SCHUSTER

THE NEW WAR

Threatens America's Security

SENATOR
JOHN KERRY

Simon & Schuster
Rockefeller Center
1230 Avenue of the Americas
New York, NY 10020

Simon & Schuster and colophon are registered trademarks
of Simon & Schuster, Inc.

Designed by Edith Fowler

Manufactured in the United States of America

10 9 8 7 6 5 4 3 2 1

Library of Congress Cataloging-In-Publication Data

Kerry, John.
The new war : the web of crime that threatens
America's security/John Kerry.
p.cm
Includes bibliographical references and index.
1.   Transnational crime. 2. Organized crime.
2.   National security.   4. National security—
United States.   I. Title.
HV6252.K47   1997
364.1'06—dc21   97-463   CIP

ISBN 0-684-84614-4

For information regarding special discounts for bulk purchases, please contact Simon & Schuster
Special Sales at 1-800-456-6798 or business@simonandschuster.com

To my parents, Richard and Rosemary, who taught me to look beyond our shores and in all directions. To my daughters, Alexandra and Vanessa, who I pray will live their adult years in a safer, more peaceful world. And to my wife, Teresa, who has brought new understanding, commitment, and meaning to my life.

Let none admire
That riches grow in Hell.

—John Milton, *Paradise Lost*,
book I, lines 690–91

Contents

Preface and Acknowledgments

In a fundamental sense, work on this book began over ten years ago. In 1985, soon after I entered the Senate, a Vietnam veteran called me with information about a group of arms-trafficking mercenaries he had met in Central America. I began investigating and stumbled into Oliver North's secret network of soldiers of fortune, arms dealers, cocaine traffickers, and corrupt officials who later became the heart of the Iran-Contra scandal. Ironically, as I write these words, that scandal has again drawn national attention, as people try to understand how some in the United States government could have allowed foreign policy objectives, like support for the Nicaraguan Contras, to facilitate the transport of illegal narcotics into the United States.

Everyone has noticed or been affected by the vast changes in our world precipitated by the end of the Cold War and the fall of the Soviet empire. The end of the bipolar East-West competition as we knew it unleashed extraordinary, complex forces that have changed the face of foreign policy—some might say forced it back into the days of more artful diplomacy.

Today everyone pays lip service to the impact of globalization and technology on our lives. But too few are acknowledging the full measure of the challenges in front of us and the steps we must take to extend our influence and protect ourselves. Neither our national response nor our vision of this new foreign policy has been adequately defined.

The prime challenges lie in five areas, all of which threaten our national security and all of which are vitally affected by the forces of the new global economy: (1) nuclear and conventional proliferation; (2) environmental degradation and crisis, with attendant issues of resource allocation and depletion; (3) fundamentalism and nationalism asserting themselves in combination through conventional conflict and terrorism; (4) the struggles of the human condition exacerbated by refugee, food, and population concerns with transboundary dislocations unprecedented in history; and (5) exploitation of all these phenomena by powerful new international criminal enterprises that threaten the stability of whole nations and challenge our standards of civilization. This book is an effort to examine the nature of this last threat, which takes advantage of every opportunity afforded it by the rapid changes of our lives.

A decade ago I began to uncover portions of a common international infrastructure for transnational crime. I saw it created in changes in the global marketplace, in computerization and globalization, in the realm of illicit arms and drug traffickers, in the world of covert action and espionage, in the networks of terrorism, in banking capitals and financial centers, in far-flung island resorts, and at ports and borders all over the world. I found that most people in the government did not have a clue as to the existence of this infrastructure or how it operated.

In the years that followed, one investigation led to another. My staff and I interviewed criminals from the inside of various U.S. prisons and found that they had had remarkable access to political figures in countries all over the world. I began tracking Colombian drug traffickers to the Bahamas and Haiti, and this work led me to the network of Manuel Noriega. Noriega's drug and intelligence network used some of the same people Oliver North had used in supplying the Nicaraguan Contras, another example of the common infrastructures of transnational crime. Some of Noriega's drug traffickers were, unfortunately, also the Contras', and for a time some of them were even employed by the United States.

In turn, the Noriega investigation opened the door to the place where he laundered his money, a bank called the Bank of Credit and Commerce International (BCCI). My investigation of BCCI, a $23 billion international financial institution, played a key role in shutting down the bank and exposing how dirty money and corruption flowed together in North American and European capitals, as well as in the developing world. The BCCI investigation took me deeper into the clandestine world of money launderers, drug traffickers, arms merchants, terrorists, and covert nuclear programs. During the dozens of hearings I held, I was able to expose a lot about this hidden world. But I felt that in the day-to-day headlines, some of the scope of what I was seeing had yet to be adequately described.

This book is an attempt to bring together that decade of work into an understandable whole. It owes its existence to the dozens of witnesses who agreed to testify before hearings I chaired; to the many others who provided critical information to me on the condition that they never be identified publicly; to the numerous officials in our government (and others) who shared their knowledge and their insights with me but cannot publicly be thanked by name; and to many members of my Senate staff who labored long hours under difficult working conditions at salaries less than they could have earned in the private sector because they believed the work mattered.

Of course, every aspect of a politician's work is collaborative. Long before a senator votes, he or she has talked to voters and constituency groups, listened to witnesses, consulted with officials and other legislators, and worked with staff to develop a position. Speeches, legislation, articles, and floor statements require expertise that no one person can have on his own, and every one of us works with lots of capable people to get our jobs done.

Every book is in some sense a collaboration between the author and the world around him. In writing this book, I have worked closely with, and must thank, a number of people. They include Helen Rees, literary agent extraordinaire, who convinced me it was important to put into one narrative the individual parts of the story she had picked up while following my career over the years; Donna Sammons Carpenter and Richard Lourie of Wordworks, who worked with me so patiently to translate my ideas, experiences, and endless sentences and paragraphs into punchy prose; and all of the supportive Wordworks team, especially Martha Lawler, who somehow orchestrated around my schedule delays during an extremely demanding election year.

I wish to also single out for special thanks the extraordinary contribution of Jonathan Winer, formerly my staff counsel, currently the deputy assistant secretary of state for law enforcement and crime. His brilliant investigative work throughout my eight years as chairman of the Subcommittee on Terrorism, Narcotics and International Operations of the Senate Foreign Relations Committee and his understanding of this issue is reflected throughout the book. Together with Jack Blum, former counsel to the Foreign Relations Committee whose tenacious, courageous work discovered BCCI's criminality, and Ron Rosenblith, my former chief of staff who first uncovered the covert networks of Central America, these former Senate staffers have helped sound an alarm of enormous importance to our law enforcement and national security communities. I am grateful for the many dinners, phone calls, and meetings that have helped produce this work.

I also want to thank my former foreign policy adviser Richard McCall, now chief of staff to US-AID, the best guide one could have had to the bureaucratic maze of the national security establishment; Frances Zwenig, my former administrative assistant and an important observer of Asian affairs; a fellow former prosecutor and POW Committee counsel, Bill Codhina; and my chief foreign policy aide, Nancy Stetson, whose values and judgment I continue to rely upon.

1

Darkness Visible

TWENTY YEARS AGO, when I ran the criminal division of the district attorney's office in urban Middlesex County, Massachusetts, small-time gangs lived like parasites off the communities, sucking protection money from small businesses and terrorizing those that hesitated to pay. Going after organized crime wasn't easy even then. Witnesses were afraid to talk. Even some law-enforcement officials could not be trusted.

The mob had infiltrated the community at a level that made rooting them out difficult. They were organized and dangerous, but they were also local boys who went all the way to New York City to get their dope—heroin through the French connection, marijuana from Mexico or Jamaica, LSD from labs in California, occasionally a little cocaine from Peru.

The drugs may have come from distant lands, but the heart of the problem remained local. If we could root these people out and send them to prison, the community would be a better place. When we finally put away Howie Winter and the top members of his notorious Winter Hill gang, who had controlled criminal activity in Somerville, Massachusetts, for decades, we knew no significant organization would replace them anytime soon.

What we didn't anticipate—what no one anticipated—was the globalization of crime, the transcontinental linking of enormous, sophisticated ethnic-based organizations. To such organizations the arrest of local operatives is of no greater significance than the capture of a few soldiers is to any army, and the seizure of a million dollars' worth of drugs can be written off with a shrug as the cost of doing business. What I learned in my eight years as chairman and two years as ranking member of the Senate Subcommittee on Terrorism, Narcotics and International Operations (now renamed the Senate Subcommittee on International Operations) is that today globalized crime can rob us not only of our money but also of our way of life.

Ten years ago few people knew about the narcoregime of General Manuel Noriega, about the dark alliance between Italy's major political parties and the mob, about the criminals who were the sidekicks to the Communist Party in the Soviet Union, or how Colombia's politicians had already begun to sell their democracy to the drug lords. Then, when I talked to other senators about transnational crime as a national security threat, the typical response was uncomprehending shoulder shrugs and shakes of the head.

Beginning in 1987, I explored the nature of the threat in public, undertaking a series of nationally broadcast hearings that described how the world's criminals had formed alliances with key officials in Central America and the Caribbean, in the Andean countries, and in Russia and nations in West Africa. These investigations, in turn, led me to the worst bank in the world, BCCI, known at the Central Intelligence Agency as the "Bank of Crooks and Criminals International." My work helped shut BCCI down, and in the process I uncovered the bad guys' links to the world of international finance and banking.

Over time, as my investigations continued, I discussed what I had found with senior officials from the CIA, the Federal Bureau of Investigation (FBI), and the Drug Enforcement Administration (DEA), as well as from British domestic and foreign intelligence (MI-5 and MI-6), and with European diplomats who gathered at Davos, Switzerland. We compared notes about the declining importance of ideology and the growing importance of mafias. We realized that cross-border international drug traffickers and money launderers, terrorists, and smugglers had become a security threat for the United States—as President Bill

Clinton announced in a speech to the United Nations General Assembly on October 22, 1995—and, indeed, for the world.

How did such a momentous change occur in so short a time? Who are the new globalized criminals and what makes their operations unlike anything we have faced before? And precisely what dangers do such lawless organizations pose to civilized society?

Origins of Globalized Crime

CRIME HAS BEEN with humanity since Cain slew Abel. And such crimes of passion will probably be with us until the world ends or man is redeemed. Organized crime also has a long lineage. Bands of thieves working together under the leadership of a chieftain like Robin Hood or Al Capone are part of both history and folklore. But Robin Hood's activities were confined to Sherwood Forest, and though he had connections with the Italian Mafia, Al Capone was Chicago-based and was undone by American law.

That has all changed. In strategy, sophistication, and reach the criminal organizations of the late twentieth century function like transnational corporations and make the gangs of the past look like mom-and-pop operations. No global enterprise, legitimate or criminal, is possible without high-level communication and logistical coordination. Today's transnational criminal cartels use high-speed modems and encrypted faxes. They buy jet airplanes three or four at a time and even have stealth-like submersibles in their armadas. They hire the finest minds to devise encryption systems and provide the complex accounting procedures any multibillion-dollar empire requires. They engage the ablest lawyers to defend them, the craftiest spin doctors to spiff their images in the media, the most persistent—and generous—lobbyists to influence legislative decisions. They retain retired intelligence officers from the world's best secret services to consult with them on security. Highly educated and well-trained scientists ensure quality control in the production of narcotics. Working with marketing people in the best traditions of the modern corporation, their research teams create new drugs like crack, the poor man's cocaine. Crack didn't just appear out of nowhere. First it was someone's idea.

Though global crime is complex and necessarily shrouded in secrecy, its sudden emergence can best be understood as part of the same great process of change that has transformed nearly all aspects of life. Rosabeth Moss Kanter, professor of business administration at Harvard Business School and prize-winning author, has said: "The American century—and the European half millennium—is coming to an end. The world century is beginning." And, I would add, the century of world crime.

What is shaping the world century are now familiar technologies—information, communications, even transportation technologies. Globalization occurred when political and technological conditions allowed for worldwide movement of information, capital, goods, and services. Crime has been globalized along with everything else except, as will be shown in some detail, our response to it.

Crime was a natural for globalization. The ability to move money electronically may be a boon for business but it is a godsend for the godfathers. The $2 trillion that zips each day through the world's banking system makes it almost impossible to trace ill-gotten gains. Transnational crime organizations immediately exploited the fall of the economic and political barriers once imposed by communism from Budapest to Beijing. Permeable borders make for a greater exchange of goods and ideas, but they also mean that more narcotics, human contraband, and even nuclear materials can slip unimpeded from place to place. The wave of democratization that swept the world in the late 1980s and early 1990s created a condition more favorable to crime than in a police state, where everyone is under tight control, free thinkers and common criminals alike. In a society riddled with informers, no large-scale conspiracy, political or criminal, has any chance of even getting past the talking stage. It is estimated, for example, that one person in four was reporting to the police in East Germany.

By its nature, crime adapts fast to changing circumstance. Unencumbered by scruple or law, criminals and criminal organizations are quick to identify new sources of profit to be had through the use of violence, deceit, or both. In some countries —for example, China—criminal organizations have a long past and traditions, but overall, these groups are still more agile than corporations and governments in adapting in-house to rapidly changing conditions in the outside world. As in any organization, criminal groups undergo generational conflicts, but they tend to be quickly and unambiguously resolved by murder, the mob's idea of downsizing.

A good many of the most serious transnational criminal organizations have been spawned by the new era. Take the Russian Mafiyas. Russia had a centuries-old tradition of outlaw groups with their own songs and symbolic tattoos; most of the people in Gulags were common criminals, not politicals or innocent victims of mass purges. But it's a long way from an old-fashioned bank robbery in Omsk or Tomsk to a Moscow mobster ordering a hit on one of his own living near the Sunset Strip in Los Angeles. The killers, former Soviet Army officers, were apprehended after cutting off the victim's fingertips and stuffing them into a Michelob beer bottle. That's globalization.

The Players

THE GLOBAL CRIMINAL AXIS is composed of five principal powers in league with a host of lesser ones, much as the Axis we faced in World War II was composed of Germany, Japan, and Italy, allied at various times with lesser powers like Hungary, Romania, and Finland. Today the Big Five are the Italian Mafia, the Russian mobs, the Japanese *yakuza*, the Chinese triads, and the Colombian cartels. They coordinate with smaller but highly organized gangs with distinct specializations in such countries as Nigeria, Poland, Jamaica, and Panama, which remains a significant narcotics transshipment and money-laundering point even after the arrest of General Noriega. These criminal alliances are still in the formative stage, but all indications are that those relations are becoming more complex and coordinated at a rapid tempo.

Christmas Day 1991, when Boris Yeltsin announced that the Soviet Union was abolished, was a momentous day for all of history, but it was also a day to remember in the long annals of crime. Communism's reign of public terror was over; in Russia and Eastern Europe, the friends of civility began to breathe freely at last. So did its enemies, and the reign of privatized terror began.

The world gazed, appalled, at one of history's most ironic twists—the transformation of a totalitarian superpower into a kleptocracy. Criminal gangs, drug cartels, racketeers, clandestine arms dealers, smugglers, scam artists, and crooked bankers moved quickly into the vacuum where the KGB and its satellite clones had been. Indeed, the KGB itself had gone private, turning from state-sponsored thuggery to something perhaps even more sinister.

Russia, it seemed, was on the verge of civil collapse, but the so-called Russian Mafiya, which included much of Russia's old KGB, was starting to flex its muscles. "It became the only organization that works in this country," one Moscow banker who uses its services told me. While the politicians and bureaucrats bickered, and the West stood by helplessly, once-disconnected gangs of thugs, thieves, and ex–intelligence officers were coalescing into powerful forces that threatened to hijack the entire country. But the Russian Mafiya had ambitions beyond beggaring its own homeland. It spread its tentacles to New York and Hong Kong, to Cyprus, Switzerland, and Italy, crowning its criminal expansion by building a heroin pipeline from the Golden Triangle of Myanmar (formerly Burma) across Asia Minor and the Balkans to Germany. Thus did a formidable new competitor claim its place as a major player in the new, and newly interconnected, global crime industry.

The '90s have seen business boom throughout that industry, with new territories and products, new strategies, alliances, and goals. The Japanese *yakuza*, which thrive on casinos, brothels, loan-sharking, corporate blackmail, and legitimate real estate, branched out to Costa Rica, São Paulo, Honolulu, Los Angeles, San Jose, and San Francisco. Their power and smarts were demonstrated in January 1995 when they, rather than the Japanese government, were first to deliver important services to the struggling survivors of the massive Kobe earthquake in their country.

Recently, when, as part of my work on the Senate Subcommittee on Terrorism, Narcotics and International Operations, we were investigating the links between the Colombian cocaine cartel, the Italian Mafia, and Polish gangsters, we interviewed a young man descended from one of Colombia's founding families. He described the cartel's investments in Caribbean banks, Panamanian shipping, Peruvian copper mines, Miami real estate, and U.S. Treasury bonds. As we talked, the young man scratched his leg, revealing a maze of bullet wounds, souvenirs of the time he refused to carry out a series of political assassinations at the request of the cartel.

What was funny about the situation, he said, was that the assassinations were hardly necessary. Colombia, he told us, was already a narcodemocracy, with bribed officials now the norm, not the exception. Increasingly, the cartel wasn't exporting just cocaine to the rest of the world, but its techniques for corruption as well. You would be amazed, he continued, at the number of officials in Western countries they had purchased. Their main goal now was to obtain respectability for their children, which is why so many are sent to the most prestigious schools in the United States. How had he become involved in the cartel? Gambling debts, he replied, very common in his social set. The United States had to understand, he added, that for many Colombians there was nothing wrong with organized crime, as long as its victims were the children of somebody else.

This aristocratic young Colombian had firsthand knowledge of the modern mob, whereas most Americans are blind to the way crime works today. Despite our near panic over the levels of violence in our country, despite our near obsession with the subject in the media, and in legislation and social policy, we don't see how crime has changed, or understand its new reach and power. The fact is that the rates for violent street crimes have declined or held steady in all major categories in recent years. Our overflowing jails can be traced to our support for growth in mandatory drug sentencing laws, which often force judges to send nonviolent first-time offenders to jail for long stretches, and siphon law-enforcement resources away from the job of locking up the hardened criminals who present a far greater threat to our society.

Much of our national hysteria on the subject can be traced to politicians who use "crime" as a code word for "race" and ride the wave of fear to victory on election day. This pandering to prejudice does a great disservice to our country, not least of all because, despite the serious impact of local crime, it closes our minds to the complex reality and imminent threat of the global crime lords and their complicity in street crime at home.

Crime still seems only a local phenomenon to most of us —terrible, terrifying, and all too familiar. We hear about our neighbor mugged in a parking lot, or see news reports about the latest shooting victim in Detroit or the dead policeman in Miami, and give thanks that we were not the victims of these random and senseless acts.

But crime today is not simply random or local; more often it is purposeful and global. The vast poppy fields in eastern Turkey are linked to the heroin dealer in downtown Detroit; the banker laundering drug money in Vienna is in league with the thriving cocaine refineries in Colombia. The men of the Chinese triads who control gambling and extortion in San Francisco's Chinatown work the same network as the Singapore gang that turns out millions of fake credit cards. The contract hit man who flies in from Moscow to kill an uncooperative store owner in New York, on behalf of the Organizatsiya, gets his fake papers by supplying the Sicilian Mafia with Soviet Army surplus ground-to-air missiles to smuggle into the Balkans to supply the Bosnian Serbs with the firepower to take on UN security forces.

The Cali cartel already has significantly compromised the Colombian government and is spreading its power internationally through alliances with the Sicilian Mafia, which has metamorphosed from a band of gangsters operating out of the chaos of postwar Sicily to an unchallenged and unchallengeable global crime syndicate. The Chinese triads, criminal corporations with ancient roots in Chinese history and modern bases in the world's Chinatowns, have mounted a campaign for supremacy in supplying the global heroin trade; the campaign was funded, in part, by the triads' profits from smuggling illegal aliens from southern China into the United States and Western Europe, where they were sold as indentured servants or put to work in the triads' sweatshops, brothels, and drug operations. Their alien smuggling operations provide a steady supply of workers for their other criminal activities because it takes years for the aliens to repay the traffickers their $30,000 fee in sweat equity.

Behind them all a worldwide banking system has evolved offshore, quasi-legal piracy cloaked in official secrecy, offering the criminal economy a safe haven to hide money from the reach of law; once laundered there, this money could then be used to infiltrate legitimate businesses and to destabilize legitimate governments—to buy judges, policemen, army officers, and government officials around the world.

Jack Blum, a lawyer specializing in the representation of victims of international crime, testified to the committee: "Surinam was, for example, for all practical purposes working for the Colombian cartels. Its central bank was the cartel window on the world financial systems. Still others offer themselves for sale as havens and waypoints." Banks, passports, and even sovereignty itself are up for sale in some countries, as we shall see at greater length in Chapter 8.

Criminals have always attempted to corrupt the social process by bribing politicians, judges, and witnesses, but they never had any intention of challenging the social order as a whole. That is not true of the new globalized crime and its fraternal twin, terrorism. Now crime often uses methods associated with terrorism, the assassination of political candidates in Colombia being only the most obvious example. And though terrorism is the use of criminal means for political or ideological ends, the distinction often blurs. It is no accident that my subcommittee investigated crime and terrorism as parts of a single sinister assault on society.

Some types of terrorists are, of course, fairly pure. The Unabomber was not out for personal gain; he only wanted to make his point, feel his power, take his pleasure. The Japanese cult Aum Shinrikyo that in March 1995 deployed poison gas in the Tokyo subways seemed to be attacking society as a whole since the cult made no attempt to wring any concessions out of it. On the other hand, the Irish Republican Army terrorists responsible for the bombings in London in February 1996 and the Hamas suicide bombers in Israel a month later were intent on wounding those societies as calculated moves in an ongoing political struggle.

However, other types of terrorists are not so easy to classify. Guerrillas, like the Shining Path in Peru, often ally themselves with organized crime, bartering passage through the territory they control in exchange for superior weaponry to use in their revolutionary assault on the government. Another example: The Montana Freemen were involved in check counterfeiting and bank fraud on a massive scale. Though they claim this was a protest against the federal government's monopoly control on currency and taxation, only subsequent investigation of the case will delineate where ideology ended and the rationale for criminality began.

Such fine distinctions mean nothing to victims. How could it possibly matter to those who have suffered wounds or grief whether the terrorists were foreign fanatics, as in the World Trade Center bombing, or homegrown, as in the bombing of the federal building in Oklahoma City and the solo strikes of the Unabomber?

But in a sense we are all victims of terrorism. Americans now must show a picture ID when flying anywhere in the country —a small loss of the freedom and ease to which we are accustomed, and, probably, worth it. But combined with other trends, like the privacy versus national security controversy that emerged over the proposed cybernetic clipper chip, treated in detail in Chapter 6, that loss of freedom reveals how terrorism and transnational crime have already begun to affect our liberties. And that's not the half of it.

The Nature of the Threat

MOST AMERICANS still refuse to believe just how well organized global crime has become. For most of us, such groups exist only in the slick fantasy world of television, movies, and thriller novels. We romanticize these outlaws, imagining they are somehow like our nostalgic, and distorted, image of the gunfighters of the

Wild West or the bootleggers of Prohibition. Like the dark and powerful men of Coppola's *Godfather* trilogy, they may thrill us or chill us, but we don't recognize them as a serious, and unprecedented, threat.

Crime has been big business for decades, of course, taking its toll in blood and corruption. But a new criminal order is being born, more organized, violent, and powerful than the world has ever seen. Its goals are more malevolent, too: It aims at nothing less than taking over entire governments.

While the American people, whipped into a frenzy by opportunistic, simplistic sloganeering and sometimes by race-baiting politicians, clamor for more prisons, three-strikes-you're-out laws, and the death penalty, forces far more powerful and insidious than street criminals threaten both our democracy and the stability of the world.

Global crime and terrorism aggressively seek to suborn institutions—the judicial process, politics, law enforcement, the media. To some extent, all this was inevitable—rival powers with conflicting interests will always clash—but it has also been a matter of deliberate policy for some criminal organizations. To quote the chillingly frank words of a Colombian crime figure who testified before the committee: "The drug business is not just money—it is also political. The head of Cali, Gilberto Rodríguez Orejuela, thinks of it as a war in which he is producing a chemical poison against the United States and its people. Since the U.S. is the only threat to him, he will do all he can to weaken the country."

At least the testimony had the virtue of honesty. And it does us an important service by putting the plain truth right in our faces. Having exhausted our rhetoric on everything from wars on poverty to wars on drugs, *we* may not think it's all-out war, but *they* do. They know exactly what it is: A war of a new kind, the whole globe its theater of operations. A war fought in thousands of small encounters every day rather than in great battles. A war between the forces of crime and the forces of civilization to determine whether crime is on the run or on the rise. It's a struggle for power, not terrain, fought more with money than with bullets, though when necessary the bullets are, of course, used.

It may well be warfare, but it's not like any we've seen

before. Then director of Central Intelligence R. James Woolsey made this point especially well when testifying before my sub-committee on April 20, 1994:

> . . . there is a major difference between the challenge posed by international crime and that posed by nations who have been our adversaries. As a rule, nations do not exist in a constant state of conflict. Even during the long struggle of the Cold War, when cooperation was not feasible, communication was possible. From quiet diplomacy to public *démarches*, from hot lines to summitry, the means could be found to try to settle disputes. Often, the negotiating table was just a phone call away.
>
> With organized crime there is no such table. The tools of diplomacy have no meaning to groups whose business revolves around drug trafficking, extortion, and murder. And when international organized crime can threaten the stability of regions and the very viability of nations, the issues are far from being exclusively in the realm of law enforcement; they also become a matter of national security.

Warfare on a global scale? A matter of national security? A skeptical reader might well ask if I'm not exaggerating for effect, to make my voice heard over the din of other warnings. But this is not only my opinion, not only Woolsey's. It is also that of President Clinton, Attorney General Janet Reno, and FBI director Louis J. Freeh. And President Yeltsin of Russia has stated that crime is the number one threat to his country's fragile democracy.

Some of the more pessimistic analysts of the Russian scene believe that a shadow government of Mafiya leaders, secret police, and corrupt politicians is already effectively running the show. But there can still be plenty of trouble without things getting that far. The economic damage and social pain caused by crime could force Russians to renounce democracy in favor of mere order, never mind the law. A Russia run by communists, fascists, or the army is unlikely to be a great friend of the United States.

And that is just a single example. Global crime poses not one but a phalanx of threats to our national security—by eroding confidence, poisoning honesty, depleting revenue; by mocking borders, currencies, passports; and, worst of all, by continually succeeding.

Besieged by a new sort of enemy in a new sort of war, we are woefully lacking in intelligence about the evolving relations among the Big Five transnational crime organizations. We do know that in the summer of 1992 the leaders of the Russian and Italian mobs held a series of secret summits in Prague, Warsaw, and Zurich. But we have yet to turn an Italian capo or a Russian thief, someone who can give us a detailed account of what transpired at those clandestine meetings. Still, the outline of their plans, and their deadly consequence, became clear within just a few months. The world's drug trade was changing, and the Russians and Italians were going to change along with it. Rather than compete, they would form a strategic alliance: The Sicilians would provide the know-how to acquire and market the drugs, and the Russians would provide security for the transit routes and distribution networks throughout the former Soviet empire.

In this new war, this "constant state of conflict" as Woolsey called it, there are a host of scenarios, few of them with happy endings.

Crime can triumph by seizing partial control of a country's presidency and congress, as it has in Colombia.

Crime can triumph by bringing down a nascent democracy like Russia, thereby throwing the international political scene into tension and turmoil.

Crime can triumph by corrupting everyone in a society— from high officials to fishermen who prefer making $10,000 a night smuggling drugs to earning $700 a week chasing thinning stocks of fish. When he was a state legislator, Abe Lincoln once threw a man out of his office who had kept upping his bribe offer. Was I still offering too little? the man asked. No, explained Lincoln, you were getting too near my price.

So, there was a good reason founding director J. Edgar Hoover fought for his entire career to keep his beloved FBI prohibited by statute from investigating drug crime. It certainly wasn't that he worried about the civil liberties issues involved, as thorny as they have always been. And it wasn't only that Hoover knew he couldn't win a war on drugs. No, the real reason was that shrewd old J. Edgar understood the risks in going after the drug trade: Drugs were poison, pretty poison—they attracted evil the way Marilyn Monroe attracted men. Drugs, he believed, could inevitably corrupt his beloved FBI.

Today, twenty-five years after Hoover's long-overdue departure, the men and women of the FBI remain largely untouched by the temptations of drug money. But that is not so true for certain precincts of the New York City Police Department, or for some cadres of police in Los Angeles, Miami, Washington, D.C., and countless other American cities and towns.

The problem is even worse outside our borders. Investigative and prosecutorial organizations around the world—from the office of the Mexican drug czar to the Russian Interior Ministry's criminal investigation department to the Colombian security police—have been tainted, subverted, or purchased outright by the billions of dollars that global crime lords are willing to spend in their search for profits.

And billions are what they have. To focus on Colombia alone, profits from the narcotics trade are estimated at close to $4 billion a year. By comparison, annual revenues from the country's largest legal export, oil, run around $1.5 billion per year. When Medellín drug lord José "the Mexican" Gonzalo Rodríguez Gacha was killed in a shoot-out with the police in Cartagena, Colombia, in 1989 and the documents of his financial empire seized, the figures were astounding. He had in Panama $22 million, Colombia $42 million, the United States $2 million, Luxembourg $39.4 million, England and Germany about $4.25 million combined, Switzerland $10.3 million, Austria $5.9 million, and Hong Kong $6 million. Even more astounding, however, was the $150 million that was found simply buried in the ground because Gonzalo had nowhere else to put it.

The only favorable scenario is the one in which we wake up to the danger to our way of life and fight global crime on its own scale. America may be both the principal market for crime and the perceived enemy of crime, but by definition it cannot be alone in the fight against criminals operating everywhere from Cali to Kiev. We should be the natural leaders of a world coalition against crime, but have yet to recognize the "new crime's" scale and sophistication.

Part of the problem is that our mentality and our legal instruments are out of date. Bill Olson, former deputy assistant secretary of state for narcotics and a fellow at the National Strategy Center in Washington, D.C., put it nicely when testifying to my subcommittee:

> ... we are dealing with an antique legal system. Our common law system, our method of prosecuting criminals, is an antique of the eighteenth century, eighteenth–nineteenth century. It is perfectly suited for the stealing of a cow on the village common. The jurisdiction is clear, you can identify what has been stolen, you can identify the villain, you can identify the victim, and you can send someone to jail.
>
> Get yourself into an international case that involves a drug cartel, an arms-smuggling ring, a bank fraud, you have got hundreds of thousands if not millions of documents in dozens of languages with many, many witnesses, many of whom are from different cultures and different backgrounds. And now you take this mess into court and you try to prosecute ... the jury is hopelessly, totally lost and confused. ... So, our legal system is really not suited for complicated international crime.

Another part of the problem is that we haven't yet gauged the true nature of the enemy's operations and the scale of his intent. As I've stated, the modern transnational criminal organization bears more than a passing resemblance to the vertically integrated corporation. But the transnational crime organization parts company with the modern corporation when it comes to dealing with the competition. The real war in Colombia was never between rival gangs. In a five-year period (between 1985 and 1990), more than a thousand police officers, over seventy journalists, some sixty judges, and an unbelievable four presidential candidates were killed by the cartels. But Colombia is only a garish and drastic example of the incessant warfare waged by crime on society.

Global crime lords are one of the greatest threats to our national security today, and to the security of a fragile globe. Why? Because it is now in their best interests to attack the institutions of society and the foundations of sovereignty, not to mention the human beings who represent those institutions and protect those foundations. Because the growth of global crime lords comes at the expense of our communities, our families, our children—our stability.

America is the great prize for criminals, the prime market for imported narcotics, weapons, and vice. For that, we are in part responsible: We create the demand for these products. Individuals must be held accountable when they buy cocaine, guns, and the services of prostitutes. But we must also recognize that the temptation to purchase is now enhanced by sophisticated organizations totally focused on the global marketing of their vicious products and violent services, and capable of the wholesale corruption of governments and societies to protect their enterprises.

America must lead an international crusade, rallying together domestically on a bipartisan basis. We must recover our courage and moral vision. The choice of futures is stark and becoming starker all the time. Either we live in a dim world of low-grade fear or we are masters in our homes, streets, and land.

America has no choice but to lead the world in the fight against "private" criminal enterprises just as we led the world in the fight against "public" criminal governments. But we cannot fight alone; we need to create a new international alliance to meet the threat, like the alliances that defeated fascism, communism, and Saddam Hussein. Our new enemies attack not by ideology or military might but by the manipulation of human weakness, greed, and despair, and by the use of atrocious violence. We will need to find new weapons to fight back, and a new will to press on with what must be a long, if not unending, struggle.

In forging an international alliance against crime, Americans will have to confront some of our most dangerous domestic demons: race, poverty, and street crime, and the often inflammatory politics that surround them. We will have to wrestle with issues that challenge our deepest beliefs about our constitutional freedoms and our appropriate international role. But success in those struggles will only make us all the more fit to lead the world into war against the sworn enemies of civilized law and human liberty.

2

Hijacking the Russian Bear

ON DECEMBER 2, 1994, at 5:30 p.m., a group of twenty men in ski masks and camouflage fatigues, armed with automatic weapons, climbed to the upper level of a parking lot in front of Moscow's city hall. As astounded Christmas shoppers and commuters watched, the hooded gunmen surrounded eight cars belonging to the MOST bank, one of Russia's most politically connected and important financial institutions. The thugs began pulling the drivers from the cars and stomping on them, breaking ribs and damaging kidneys in the process.

That night Russian president Boris Yeltsin called for an investigation, as did Moscow's mayor, Yuri Luzhkov. Weeks passed, and no explanation was ever offered.

Recently, over dinner, a Kremlinologist friend of mine explained this bizarre event to me as just another manifestation of the struggle between the mobs and the government. MOST wasn't just a bank, he said, but home to many former KGB officials who were aligned with Mayor Luzhkov against the Yeltsin forces. Luzhkov, who associates with corrupt officials and gangsters in Russia, had been depositing government funds in the bank, which in turn had been using the money to buy up major Russian newspapers, and television and radio stations, in a clear prelude to a power grab by the mayor. MOST also had its own security service of a thousand men, and had recently been linked to an assault on the ruble that sent its international value plummeting. It is widely speculated that the ruble manipulations had enriched MOST at the same time they damaged the Russian economy and weakened the Yeltsin government. The press suggested that the MOST raid was likely a message from Yeltsin to Luzhkov that Yeltsin was still in charge. It wasn't yet clear how MOST would retaliate, but my friend assured me that its thugs were every bit as tough as any employed by the Russian government.

I wondered whether Yeltsin would approve of the tactics of kidney crushing and rib bashing by men in ski masks. The Kremlinologist explained that Yeltsin might even have authorized the raid, but he probably didn't control it. "You can't think about the battle for Russia's future as a struggle between political parties," he said. "It's more like a Mafiya gang war, and anything can happen after Yeltsin."

Lulled by more than two hundred years of successful democracy, many Americans have difficulty grasping the enormity of the threat posed by the global crime lords' relentless drive to gain control of the very institutions that hold society intact. They aim at nothing less than the dominance of civil society.

It is comforting for the diplomats, economists, and businesspeople who watch from the West to imagine that the current chaos in Russia is just a stage, one step in the transformation of the so-called evil empire into a free-market democracy. "Robber capitalism," George Soros, one of our era's most successful capitalists, calls it, a period not unlike the hurly-burly twenty years after our own Civil War when colossal fortunes were amassed in a business climate free of regulation.

What's happening in Russia today is more than simple frontier-style robbery, however. It is the hijacking of a nation's entire economy by increasingly organized criminal groups, through systematic racketeering, murder, fraud, auto theft, assault, drug distribution, trafficking in weapons and radioactive material, prostitution, smuggling, extortion, embezzlement, and the infiltration and purchase of Russian banks. Russia's criminal class has evolved from the black marketers, minor thugs, and fixers that existed at the fringe of the old Soviet state into the sophisticated power brokers and moneymen who are pushing a once vast and powerful empire into wholesale criminality and corruption.

Russians describe the current period as a *smuta*, or "time of troubles": a chaotic interregnum like that of the early seventeenth—and twentieth—century, when anarchy ended only with the establishment of yet another autocracy. Russia is going through a revolution, a depression, and a gold rush simultaneously. Everything is up for grabs, and might makes right.

For the average Russian, life is harder now than it ever was under the old system: Beggars crowd the subway stops in Moscow, and famine stalks the once productive mill cities of Siberia and the Urals. Street crime is everywhere; news of murders, muggings, and robberies dominate the newspapers and television reports. In a country reduced to economic ruin, crime is the obvious path to quick money; and in a country of many unassimilated ethnic groups, it is an obvious expression of alienation and revenge.

Corruption, of course, was endemic under communism, the grease that kept the old command economy creaking along. Anything was available, for a price, on the black market; any problem could be fixed, usually with a bottle of vodka. But the criminals were marginal; exercising no power, they were mere servants of the power elite known as the nomenklatura, and forever at risk of incarceration or worse at the hands of the secret police.

With the end of empire, those checks disappeared, however. Sensing communism's demise, the KGB stole billions in party funds and stashed them abroad, under the control of con men whose release they obtained from Soviet prisons. In partnership, these ex–intelligence agents and felons had the skills and the ruthlessness to thrive in the chaos—and the money and connections to convince many former apparatchiks and KGB veterans to join their cause.

As time passes, it becomes harder and harder to distinguish parts of the Russian government from the Russian mob. The army has used its special assassination squads to train hit men for the mob, even as the mob opens foreign bank accounts for senior government officials. The regime of public terror deployed by the Soviet state under Vladimir Lenin and Joseph Stalin has gone private, its oppressiveness on ordinary people moderated only by the fact that rival gangs save much of their murderous fury for each other.

As the mafiosi have grown, they have changed. Originally disconnected groups, now they have coalesced into a federation of sorts. Originally they were simple extortionists, threatening businesses with a beating or a bombing unless they were paid for protection. Now they demand a piece of the business itself, along with control of the profit. Russian government officials tell me that some 90 percent of the nation's businesses have some Mafiya ties, and 40 percent are totally Mafiya controlled. They have penetrated the banks and control much of the country's dwindling capital; the money is spent in currency speculation, used to fund arms and narcotics trafficking, or used to buy multimillion-dollar lakefront villas in Geneva.

Organized crime's theft of the Russian economy dooms any attempts at market reform before they have even been given a chance. But as Yeltsin has publicly acknowledged, the Mafiya is also "the single greatest threat" to the survival of Russian democracy, a statement underscored by the Mafiya contract killing on October 17, 1994, of Dmitri Kholodov, a Moscow investigative reporter who had been probing high-level corruption within the Russian armed forces. It was not only my Kremlinologist friend but also many other Western experts who feared that because of organized crime Yeltsin would not only be Russia's first democratically elected leader, but its last as well. Those fears, fortunately, have so far proved unfounded, at least as far as Yeltsin's reelection was concerned. The sources of those fears—the corruption, the violence, the sense of flagrant injustice—continue to threaten Russia's political stability.

As the Russian people sink further into Third World penury, afraid to walk the streets after dark, watching the mafiosi and their partners in the nomenklatura drive by in Rolls or Mercedes, their anger rises. So do calls for a strongman to take control of the chaos: Not a wealthy member of the elite like Yeltsin's prime minister, Viktor Chernomyrdin, grown rich from Russian privatization, nor even one of the discredited communists like Gennadi Zyuganov. Rather, as in France after the revolutionary fervors had cooled into ordinary greed, a military man like General Alexander Lebed may appear as the man on horseback, ready to vanquish the forces of disorder. Already, General Lebed—who was anointed in June 1996 by Yeltsin as Russia's national security adviser and fired just four months later—has begun to play the patriotic populist-nationalist chords that have led to so many of the world's armed conflicts.

Crime's Deep Roots

How DID THINGS DETERIORATE so quickly after the heady days of champagne parties on the Berlin wall and the lowering of the red flag on the Kremlin in December 1991? As a brief glance into Russia's past shows, the current criminal chaos was a long time in the making.

In Western democracies, "law and order" are said in a single breath like "ham and eggs." But in Russia, the two ideas are quite separate, and for good reason. There is a deep-seated cynicism toward the law among the common people—they had no say in the creation of the laws and those laws rarely if ever worked for their betterment. A common proverb compares the law to a cart whose direction depends entirely on who is in the driver's seat.

The early revolutionaries had absolutely no respect for the law and considered every assault on it a blow struck for justice. They engaged in the usual acts associated with terrorism, like the assassination of police officers, high officials, and the royal family (Czar Alexander II was killed by a bomb hurled at his carriage in 1881). But the revolutionaries took the usual practices one step further. Operating on Lenin's principle of "expropriating the expropriated" (stealing back what had been stolen from the people), they staged a series of dramatic and successful bank robberies that would in one blow shatter the confidence of czarist society and fill the coffers of the revolutionaries. Stalin is believed to have been behind the biggest bank job of all time in Russia. Lenin found him particularly valuable for that—Stalin didn't engage in hair-splitting theoretical debates, he got things done.

Under the communists, Russia was doubly corrupt. The government, especially under Stalin, was simply a criminal organization that unleashed unprecedented violence against the population, always justified by laws passed by the rubber-stamp parliament. Except in petty matters, nearly all trials were show trials. Furthermore, the population itself was also "criminalized." By nationalizing all property and by outlawing nearly all forms of private enterprise, the government forced the Soviet people to choose among a life of honest misery, severe punishment (many so-called economic crimes were punishable by death), and the sort of petty larceny and graft that became endemic.

Though the Soviets pretended that crime was a manifestation of the inequalities fostered by capitalism, crime was still rife in Soviet society. This included the usual acts of violence like assault, rape, and murder, as well as the crimes that result from state control of the economy—black marketeering, trading in foreign currencies. Bribery and corruption were all-pervasive. Fortunes were paid to government officials in charge of scarce resources. And if a nurse didn't find a ruble under a patient's pillow his bedsheets wouldn't be changed.

If any Russians still harbored illusions about the sort of society they lived in, the revelations that occurred during Mikhail Gorbachev's period of glasnost dispelled them once and for all. The public was bombarded with information on everything from the grisly murder of Czar Nicholas II and the royal family in 1918 to the exact extent of Stalin's murders to the lavish privileges enjoyed by the power elite behind well-guarded fences in secluded retreats. The elite dined on sturgeon and caviar while the average Russian scraped by on potatoes, black bread, and tea. Their slightest ailment was treated with rare and costly medicines from abroad while for the average Russian aspirin tablets were as precious as pearls and the free socialist medical system supplied root canals at no charge but without anesthesia either.

It was into this moral vacuum that Russian democracy and the free market were born. The miracle is that they took root to the extent that they did. A rough-and-tumble sense of democracy has emerged among the Russian citizenry, who have defied the skeptics time and again both to turn out to vote in larger numbers than anticipated and to support candidates, like General Lebed, the pundits failed to predict. And the Russians have also demonstrated a flair for entrepreneurship that seemed to have been frozen in a state of suspended animation for more than seventy years, thriving exclusively within the limits of the black market, which, I learned on a visit to Moscow, was entrepreneurial in the best capitalist tradition. But both the free market and the free society are threatened by the emergence of the Mafiyas.

Who are they and how do they operate?

In the Soviet period, "real" crime was committed by loosely organized gangs of professionals whose hands, arms, and sometimes entire bodies were covered with elaborate and symbolic tattoos. Usually obtained in prison, a mix of urine, ballpoint ink, and the ash of burned shoe heels, the tattoos provide more information about a criminal than a rap sheet: A leopard with bared teeth or a skull split by lightning with the caption "KILLER KOMMANDO," in English, indicates a professional assassin; epaulets indicate a prison camp enforcer; a spiderweb means a drug trafficker; an eight-pointed star signifies a professional thief.

For the most part, their operations were necessarily small-time. The state was jealous of its power, and strict controls were enforced on weapons, transportation, and communication. It was almost impossible for a Soviet citizen to own a rifle unless he was a member of an officially sponsored hunting organization, phones were routinely bugged, and vehicles, whether trucks or cars, were largely unavailable for private use. Like everything else, the banks were state-owned and -controlled, making any money laundering quite out of the question. The Russian criminal caste may have been colorful, but they posed only a minor inconvenience to society. Break-ins were rare and the streets were safe. The real criminals were in the government and the Communist Party.

All that changed with the fall of communism. Not only was there a moral vacuum, but everything was up for grabs. The difference between the winners and the losers was going to be immense. In the Soviet period, most people lived in what could be called a "democracy of poverty," and the lush life of the leaders was carefully screened from public view. Now the new rich— identified in the public mind with crime lords—flaunt their wealth. In Soviet times, luxury items were available only to the power elite. They shopped in special stores that were never open to the public but only to those few members of the Communist Party who were sufficiently trusted to travel abroad (and who shipped everything from modern bathroom facilities to Pierre Cardin clothing back home). Now all that too has changed. All the big-name international companies have opened branches in the major Russian cities, and street kiosks offer the low end of luxury goods, though in many cases these are fakes, and in the case of some supposed French cognacs proved lethal to unsuspecting customers. Amaretto, the producer of Italian liqueurs, has issued a warning that as much as 70 percent of what passes as its product in Russia is no more than crude moonshine.

The new order tempts everyone to criminality. Just as in America, the street punk impatient for sneakers, drugs, or gold chains performs the kind of quick and violent crime that erodes the quality of daily life and makes people yearn for order. The scientist, finding himself underpaid and without social status, is tempted to work for criminal organizations in enterprises that range from creating communication systems to preparing fissionable materials for explosive devices. Officers in the Russian Army, demoralized by defeats in Afghanistan and Chechnya, living on a pittance, often without even adequate housing, are natural recruits for the Mafiyas. Some are valuable to the crime lords while remaining in the army, where they can siphon off gas, vehicles, and weapons—even missile launchers have been reported missing. Others are better put to work in the direct service of organized crime as hit men. Some of the recent assassinations in Russia have clearly been the work of army-trained snipers. For decades communist leaders exhorted their people to "overtake and surpass" the United States. It finally happened in 1993, when Russia's murder rate hit eighty a day, beating the United States by a good ten.

Low-paid police and customs officials are easy targets for bribery. Even before the fall of communism, Alexander Gurov, head of the Soviet Interior Ministry's Sixth Department to Combat Organized Crime, estimated that four out of five policemen were on the take. That was then. And now? "Corruption is devouring the state from top to bottom," said President Yeltsin.

But those are the small fry, the rank and file. The real

power lies with the Russian godfathers and their allies—former KGB officials with important positions in the sectors of the economy, whether privatized or still under state control, and corrupt politicians in high office. Together they form what has been called a shadow government, one not involved in the day-to-day business of running the country, but with effective control of key areas of the economy. Former KGB general Oleg Kalugin, now a frequent guest on American TV talk shows, has said: ". . . if you make our economy a normal market economy, the shadow structure will simply evaporate into it."

But that's a big "if" when a great deal of everything, from the smallest business to the state enterprises that control the country's mineral wealth, is under Mafiya command. Every Russian city has been carved up by mobs according to specialty— drugs, prostitution, slot machines. Russia has become a major conduit and distributor of opium poppy grown in the Central Asian states as well as of heroin from Iran, Pakistan, and Afghanistan. The war in the former Yugoslavia disrupted one of the main distribution links for drugs from the East, providing Russia with an opportunity to muscle in. Russian heroin, speed, PCP, crack, and designer drugs are mostly feeding some 1.5 million new addicts in Russia, but distribution networks are already expanding into Germany and the rest of Europe, with the United States a likely target in the near future.

In January 1993 authorities seized more than a metric ton of cocaine in St. Petersburg, the first indication that Russia had also become an important transshipment point for drugs, most of which arrive on the regularly scheduled flights from South America and then move out through Russia's 36,000 miles of border. By the end of 1993, narcotics seizures in Russia totaled 35 tons. Two years later Russian law enforcement reported that a total of 90 tons of illicit narcotics had been seized.

Russia proper—as opposed to Central Asia—has become both a producer and a market for drugs. Marijuana grows wild in Siberia and southern Russia, covering some 2.4 million acres, roughly the size of Connecticut. Two hundred fifteen illicit laboratories producing amphetamines were seized in 1993. In addition, the Russians are creating synthetic drugs—Crocodile and Devil—reputed to be a thousand times more powerful than heroin. Some of these laboratories are located in formerly state-supported, now impoverished universities. Estimates of the number of addicts in Russia itself range from 1.5 million to 6 million, with Russian authorities claiming that drug use there was increasing by 50 percent a year as of the end of 1995.

Another area where the Russian mobs have been particularly active—and particularly damaging to the country's economy—is in the illicit purchase and sale of natural resources. As Stephen Handelman, a visiting scholar at Columbia University's Harriman Institute and former Moscow bureau chief of the *Toronto Star*, writes in *Foreign Affairs* magazine:

> . . . the smuggling trade flourished as enormous quantities of copper, zinc and other strategic metals were shipped from central Russia in unmarked trucks or military aircraft to Baltic ports and then to Scandinavia or Western Europe. The smugglers took brilliant advantage of the Commonwealth clash of sovereignties: products stolen from a Russian factory were regarded as legal goods the moment they left Russia's borders. So much illicit metal from Russian defense factories passed through Estonia on its way overseas—an estimated half a million dollars' worth a day in 1992—that the tiny Baltic republic earned the distinction of being one of the world's largest exporters of finished metal without operating a single metal plant.

But perhaps the greatest threat to Russia's nascent free-market economy is posed by the protection money the Mafiyas extort from nearly every business. The choice they offer is stark and simple: Pay or die. A Russian woman, a former physics teacher with two children to raise on her own, opened a small cafe that quickly became an in spot frequented by artists, journalists, and local pop music stars. Then, she related, "These two fellows came into my cafe. One reminded me in a quiet whisper that I have two kids, and he whispered my address. Then we went into the kitchen, where they laid out all of the kitchen tools —the knives, the cleavers, the mallets. They told me to choose the weapon they would use to kill me if I said no."

The woman's cafe is all of Russia's fledgling economy in

miniature. A government report prepared for President Yeltsin estimated that 70 to 80 percent of private enterprises and commercial banks in all the major cities were paying 10 to 20 percent of their income to organized crime in exchange for protection. Even if we take the most conservative side of these figures—70 percent of businesses paying 10 percent—it still means that an astonishing 7 percent of the country's privately produced income flows right off the top into the pockets of organized crime. Some estimates place mob control of Russia's total gross national product at somewhere between 30 and 40 percent.

Most people, but not all, prefer to pay rather than die. In 1995 some two dozen bankers were shot dead by professional criminals, or those trained to kill by the military or secret police. The most shocking killing was that of Nikolai Likhachev, chairman of the Russian Agricultural Bank, who was gunned down in the lobby of his apartment building at close range, shot with a revolver apparently outfitted with a silencer. Likhachev was known to be scrupulously honest and his murder, still unsolved, puzzled the Russian financial community. Was it the result of a failed extortion attempt? Or was it a generalized warning to the banking community? And was there any truth to the rumors that the order for the hit had come not from Moscow but New York?

But the 7 percent or more the mob siphons off the economy doesn't stay in its pockets. The mob invests. It's both a way to get a piece of the legitimate action and a perfect way to launder money. And there's no better business for laundering money than your own private bank. Of course, no one knows with certainty how many of Russia's banks are controlled or even owned by the mob. In 1994, Alexei Belov, deputy head of the Interior Ministry's criminal investigation department, knew precisely how many banks Russia had—2,048—but was considerably less precise when it came to mob involvement: "A big proportion of our banks are linked to mafia and criminal gangs. What percentage I cannot say."

The deputy head of currency control at the central bank, Vladimir Smirnov, has stated: "We know that some banks employ former convicts and criminals who have spent time in jail. But it is not up to the central bank to deal with this sort of problem." Russia's state-controlled socialist economy never had the slightest need to develop a complex banking code or the trained people to enforce it. Such laws and such people are not created overnight. In the meantime, Russia and some of the East European countries have become major money-laundering centers, thereby providing a service they can sell to an increasingly specialized international criminal community. The first major attempt at money laundering, in the wildest period of "Wild East" capitalism in 1992, was aborted but nevertheless provides a good sense of the scale on which the globalized crime organizations now operate. The scam: The Russian banks would swap $7.8 billion of American and Sicilian Mafia money for 140 billion rubles. This would allow Westerners to buy Russian natural resources and sell them in the West at three hundred to four hundred times the original investment.

Russian officials have estimated that capital leaving Russia controlled by politicians, mafiosi, and Russian businessmen totaled $300 billion during the first two years of post-perestroika capitalism (1992 through 1994). Russian mobsters have learned fast to diversify their holdings; besides, they know as well as anyone else what an unpredictable country they live in. One of the popular chords sounded by the hard-liner Vladimir Zhirinovsky was his call for "on the spot execution of criminal gang leaders by firing squads . . . I will immediately declare a dictatorship. I may have to shoot 100,000 people, but the other 300 million will live peacefully. I have the right to shoot these 100,000. I have this right as president."

For American law officials to arrest and execute that number of people would be a ruinous social trauma. In this century in Russia such events have been all too common. President Yeltsin's uncertain health and questions about who will succeed him provide the mob all the more reason to remove its money from circulation in Russia. Foreign investors are not likely to see Russia as an attractive place to put their money when both legitimate businessmen and criminals are shipping its money out and social conditions offer little hope of incipient stability. Between 1987 and 1993, U.S. companies invested an average of only $60 million per year in Russia. But according to CIA director John Deutch, extortion from an estimated 70 to 80 percent of private businesses by the Russian mob has jeopardized continued U.S.

investment in Russia. Foreign businesspeople are routinely threatened and find little cooperation from local police and courts. Codorníu, the Spanish wine company, was robbed of a hundred truckloads of its produce in a single night from a warehouse in St. Petersburg. When the Spaniards turned for help to the "economic crimes" branch of the police, they were given the phone number and address of "certain people in St. Petersburg who might be able to help you." Those people turned out to be the gangsters who had commandeered the wine in the first place. American investors in the Subway sandwich chain had a similarly unpleasant experience when their partners locked them out of their Russian venture amid death threats. The intimidation of foreign investors further weakens the economy, and that in turn makes the appeal of extreme politicians stronger. It's a fateful dynamic, a death embrace.

On November 3, 1996, the truth of this fact hit the American business community in Moscow when thirty-nine-year-old Paul Tatum from Oklahoma was murdered at the entrance to a Moscow subway close to the state-of-the-art Radisson hotel he had created in a joint venture involving the Moscow city government. Tatum was killed by eleven bullets from a machine gun wrapped in plastic and left at the scene by professional hit men. Over the previous two years he had been involved in a bitter dispute with his Russian business partners and spent much of the time locked in the Moscow Radisson, in defiance of his partners' warnings that if he did not leave Russia they would kill him. Tatum wrongly believed no one would dare hurt him, given his close ties to important figures in the Republican Party in the United States and the high profile of his hotel, which is considered the finest in Moscow and is the place where President Clinton and many other dignitaries stay when they are in town. But as one of Tatum's American colleagues in Moscow told me, in becoming partners with the city of Moscow, Tatum had let a cat into the business, and the cat not only had claws, it was a panther whose laws were those of the jungle. Tatum's friends say they know who ordered the murder, but they are sure it will remain unsolved, like so many similar killings in today's Moscow.

A Global Threat

WHAT AMERICA MUST REALIZE is that the success of Russian democracy is intimately connected with the success of the free market. Unlike the Chinese, who took it one step at a time—reforming the economy but leaving the political structure alone—the Russians have gambled on both democracy and capitalism, and they have to win on both.

America's own interests are clearly better served by a democratic, capitalist Russia than one run by communists, fascists, the military, or the mafiosi. Since Russia remains a large and important country—still the number two nuclear power—it is entirely in our national security interests to see political and economic freedom flourish there. History shows that democracies tend to be allies rather than enemies.

In the months preceding the Russian presidential elections in June 1996, American politicians and commentators did a lot of hand-wringing about whether or not Yeltsin, or some other progressive candidate, should be openly or indirectly supported. In fact, some very real as well as some valuable symbolic gestures were made. On February 22 the International Monetary Fund granted Russia a $10 billion loan. In April, President Clinton attended a summit in Moscow with Yeltsin. But as we know from Gorbachev, respect abroad does not always translate into respect at home.

In any case, while shoring up the more progressive of Russia's politicians will continue to be our goal, they will prove ineffective unless they can break crime's stranglehold on the Russian economy without destroying everything worthwhile the country has gained in the five short years since communism fell.

Just by itself, that stranglehold on the economy is bad enough. But when coupled with infiltration of the political process, it becomes doubly lethal. Says Stephen Handelman: "The Russian mafiya's connection with government, born of its symbiotic relationship with the former communist establishment, makes organized crime a dagger pointed at the heart of Russian democracy."

By remaining the principal enemy of Russian democracy, Russian criminal organizations remain a threat to our national security and must be both perceived as such and then acted upon. To take a hypothetical example, it makes more sense to give Russian law-enforcement agencies 10,000 computers than it does to distribute them in the private sector.

There is absolutely no question that the Russian mobs are miles ahead of law enforcement in every department—they have superior weapons, vehicles, and communications. The mob drives Mercedes that are stolen by the thousands in Western Europe and shipped straight to Russia. In some cases, the police are forced to flag down cabs to chase criminals; some are even reduced to taking the bus to crime scenes. "We perform autopsies with kitchen knives," complained Colonel Yuri Dubyagin in a morgue outside Moscow whose floor, made of packed dirt and caked with blood, was piled with the tattooed corpses of criminals. To compound matters, Russian gangs continue to operate across the entire territory of the former Soviet Union, which has in the meantime split into some fifteen countries. Cooperation and coordination among those countries are poor for a variety of reasons—lingering ill will toward Russia; a multitude of national languages that have replaced Russian, the lingua franca of the former USSR; and the usual lack of resources.

As we have seen, by jeopardizing the country's experiment with freedom, Russian criminal organizations pose a threat to our national security. However, that threat is not limited to the damage crime can do to Russia's free market and democratic process. Its links with the Italian Mafia in the transshipment of narcotics have made the Russian mobs major players on the international scene. They are now an essential component in the system that runs from the poppy fields of Central Asia to the vein in a junkie's arm in any of a thousand American cities and towns. As the arrest of Russian mobster Boris Nayfeld has shown, the heroin connection was itself financed by deals between the mafiosi and corrupt Soviet Army officials who sold off a fortune in stolen military equipment and weapons.

The Mafiya delivery system, which can supply arms as well as drugs, has also alarmed our European allies. David Veness, head of Scotland Yard's specialist CID unit on organized crime, predicted in 1993 that within five years gangsters from Eastern Europe and the former Soviet Union would become the biggest suppliers of guns and drugs to Britain's inner cities. He's been proved all too right. Shipments of Russian and Polish arms have been seized en route to the IRA and have been found in the arsenals of the Italian Mafia and the Islamic Jihad.

The Germans are worried too. Hans-Ludwig Zachert, head of the Bundeskriminalamt, Germany's federal police agency, calls organized crime "public enemy number one" and describes Germany today not so much as "multicultural" as "multicriminal." The Turks run the drug business; the Poles and Romanians specialize in car theft (63,000 vehicles were stolen in Germany in the first six months of 1992); the Yugoslavs are in charge of pimping and the Italians of money laundering. And the 300,000 former Soviet citizens in Berlin have begun to make their presence felt. Russian mobsters have been arrested in Germany for extortion, car theft, counterfeiting, prostitution, selling drugs and illegal weapons, and smuggling everything from icons to uranium.

Europeans are worried for good reason, says Boris Uvarov, chief investigator of major crime for the Russian attorney general: "It's wonderful that the Iron Curtain is gone, but it was a shield for the West. Now we've opened the gates, and this is very dangerous for the world. America is getting Russian criminals; Europe is getting Russian criminals. They'll steal everything. They'll *occupy* Europe. Nobody will have the resources to stop them. You people in the West don't know our mafia yet; you will, you will."

There is no question that in America Russian criminals have become increasingly active coast to coast. These criminals include both those who emigrated to this country and those based in Russia itself but with transnational operations. As we've seen, Russian mob violence is a two-way street. A hit in Los Angeles can be called in Moscow, and Brooklyn can return the favor in St. Petersburg. To get a sense of how quickly Russian crime is infiltrating the United States, it was only two years from the time that communism officially fell in Russia, December 25, 1991, until December 1993, when Attorney General Janet Reno raised the Russian Mafiya to a Justice Department enforcement priority alongside traditional Sicilian-connected organized crime and Asian drug-trafficking gangs.

First centered in New York City's Brighton Beach, the traditional landing point for Russian immigrants, the Russian

Mafiya began by copying the simple business extortion techniques it had used in Moscow. Today, however, it is a sophisticated competitor here as well: "The fastest-growing criminal organization in the United States," FBI director Louis J. Freeh told the Congress.

Among the groups identified by the FBI so far: the Organizatsiya, centered in Brighton Beach and specializing in fraudulent tax schemes and illegal immigration; the West Coast Russian Group, specialists in money laundering through Russia to Finland, Singapore, Germany, the United States, and the Cayman Islands; and the Russian-Armenian Mafiya, based in New York and Southern California, which smuggles weapons, controls prostitution, and carries out murder for hire.

In keeping with the modern trend toward specialization, Russian crime in the United States falls into certain definite areas. One favorite is the bootlegging of gasoline, using dummy corporations to defraud the government of over a billion dollars a year in tax revenues. Gasoline merchants who were reluctant to cooperate in those schemes have been subjected to threat and force. Other types of complex fraud are also favored, especially staged auto accidents and false medical billing schemes. In one of the largest cases of its kind, in 1994 the U.S. attorney's office in Los Angeles brought a 175-count indictment against a gang headed by two Russian émigrés, Michael and David Smushkevich, brothers charged with bilking $1 billion from insurance companies by using rolling medical labs to conduct fake tests on patients, then submitting hugely inflated bills. Michael Smushkevich pled guilty to money laundering and was sentenced to twenty-one years. The importance of documents—the so-called internal passports required for travel from city to city—in the former Soviet Union produced a whole caste of expert forgers who have now transferred their skills to this country. As far back as the late '80s, Russian émigré mobsters were counterfeiting American currency and American Express traveler's checks. They have also dealt in bogus Fabergé jewels. In addition, the Russians have branched out into prostitution and loan-sharking, and are deeply involved in the importing of heroin and opium from Central Asia and the Golden Triangle into this country.

The Russian national police warn that poppy and marijuana from Central Asia and the Caucasus are flooding the former Soviet Union. In St. Petersburg alone, the number of officially registered addicts of hard drugs has reached 300,000, or almost one in fifteen of the city's entire population. As Russian police colonel Vladimir Rakitan, head of anti-narcotics efforts in Murmansk, told a Russian newspaper in March 1996, "Russia attracts the criminal clan of the entire world as a boundless market for selling drugs." While Russian authorities were able to seize 90 metric tons of narcotics in 1995, Russian law-enforcement officials believe this is just a fraction of the amount that gets through. One measure of the size of the trade is the continuing export of some $1.5 billion by criminals out of Russia to the West every month, according to the Russian Ministry of the Interior.

As an example of our failure to treat the globalization of crime with appropriate seriousness, it took until 1994 for the FBI to open an office in Moscow. As we shall see in Chapter 9, that office has scored impressive successes in a very short time. But the FBI Moscow office has also been stonewalled when it attempted to investigate people with strong, close connections to those in office. Here at home we are still hampered by a lack of personnel familiar with the intricacies of Russian crime, not to mention the language. It took federal investigators years to penetrate the north New Jersey gas tax frauds that married the Italians and the Russians in a billion-dollar regional crime enterprise. By the time the original gangs were indicted, clones of their operations had spread coast to coast and become a multibillion-dollar industry.

Though the increase of Russian crime in our country can hardly be viewed as a favorable development, it does not alone constitute a danger to our national security. But Russian crime's successes here are a reflection of its growth and power in Russia, and as such of its growing part in the overall threat posed by globalized crime. The greatest danger to us comes from the damage that crime can do to Russia's economy, and therefore to its stability and fight for democracy. Criminal activity has replaced communism as our enemy in Russia. But there is yet one other serious hazard, as we shall see in Chapter 6 when we consider how the unused nuclear materials of the Cold War can become weapons for global criminals in their new hot war against our law, liberty, and institutions.

3

China on the Brink

THE MOST CORRUPT SOCIETY on earth," was what one expert witness before my subcommittee called China. And though corruption is hard to measure, China clearly has a problem.

There is a Chinese term for a system of corruption, *guanxi*, which essentially boils down to the principle of "you scratch my back and I'll scratch yours." *Guanxi* comes from a Mandarin expression translated by Chinese crime expert Willard Myers III as "I have many friends." Under the *guanxi* system of Chinese capitalism, everyone trades favors, sharing their network of contacts with whoever is in need. Is a customs declaration needed to ship illicit arms? My *guanxi* friend will take care of your need, receiving a "chit" from me for a favor to be named later, even as I, who work in, say, the police or Foreign Affairs Ministry, receive a "chit" from you. Informal networks of *guanxi* thus exist throughout the land—a system of hidden relationships to get things done, regardless of whether the activity happens to be legal.

This system of corruption is eating away at the structures that provide stability in China today. So far the Communist Party has proved to be both stable and adaptable, but we have already seen in recent years a good many examples of the sudden swiftness with which communist societies can collapse.

This growing corruption means a complete blurring of

the distinctions among business, crime, and government. Previously, all actions that served the party were justifiable. Now all actions that serve the cause of profit are equally justifiable. The theft of state resources, the bribing of officials, the smuggling of aliens and narcotics, and legitimate business all blend into one in the striving to fulfill the dictum of recently deceased Paramount Leader Deng Xiaoping: "To get rich is glorious."

China's authoritarian government struggles with the mere task of maintaining order as opposed to the larger task of teaching moral values. And there are few social forces apart from the family with the authority to create moral values. By admitting that the economic foundation of its political philosophy was wrong—by allowing the demonstration that capitalism is superior to socialism—the party no longer could claim the same moral legitimacy. But it did have the advantages of guns and incumbency.

Essentially, Chinese leaders have struck a compromise. No longer driven by pure ideology, they remain in power to provide both the continuity and the stability required for powerful economic progress. But sooner or later the compromise will be tested—possibly as soon as the lease runs out on Hong Kong.

In the meantime, corruption is so rife that as far back as August 1993 the Central Committee of the Chinese Communist Party complained that the "Army and armed police have abused their prerogatives to smuggle goods." This is a startling statement. Even more startling was the revelation, confirmed in 1993 in Beijing by Public Security Minister Tao Siju, that some high Chinese officials rely on the Hong Kong–based Sun Yee On Triad to protect them during travels abroad. Sun Yee On, which means New Righteousness and Peace, is the largest (56,000 members), most tightly structured, and most powerful of the triads, as Chinese criminal organizations are called. It specializes in extortion, heroin trafficking, and alien smuggling, in a net that extends to Canada, Australia, Thailand, and Central America. Under the circumstances, just what are we to make of Minister Tao's comment in April 1996 that he considers Sun Yee On to be a "patriotic" organization? It would probably be wisest to simply take him literally.

International criminal forces have fostered a growth industry in lower-tier corruption among Chinese officialdom. A large-scale alien smuggling organization based in Guangzhou takes official Chinese passports issued by the Chinese government for businessmen to promote Chinese commerce and provides them to smugglers for $15,000 each, together with visas and phony invitations from American businesses to come to the United States.

A growing black market in small arms, including military weapons, in Yunnan Province and Guangxi, bordering the Golden Triangle, feeds off the needs of the heroin armies of the Golden Triangle. Further afield, breaking the UN international embargo on arms sales to the ethnic combatants in the former Yugoslavia, Chinese arms merchants became key suppliers.

Some Chinese were blasé about the early signs of crime and corruption, taking refuge in the old saying "When you open the window, some flies will come in." But they came in by the swarm. In China as a whole, violent crime jumped 15.6 percent between 1993 and 1994. Robbery was up 14.9 percent, fraud by 26 percent, and theft by 17.7 percent. Even in Beijing, 4,300 manhole covers were stolen, apparently for their scrap value. But those figures were dwarfed in the Shenzhen Special Economic Zone in the south, where China's experiment with capitalism had been first introduced. There crime rose 66 percent in that same period while prostitution, gambling, and drug abuse convictions rose 92 percent.

The Chinese market for criminal activity is now growing along with everything else in that high-powered economy, which steamed along at an annual growth rate of 10.2 percent in the first quarter of 1996. Earlier in 1996, China crime expert Willard Myers III estimated yearly Chinese earnings from drug production, smuggling, and distribution alone at more than $200 billion; alien smuggling at more than $3.2 billion; weapons smuggling at more than $3 billion; and smuggling of cars, boats, and electronics at more than $4 billion.

Some parts of the Chinese system fight back at crime. In 1995 the police mounted a serious anti-crime drive in the economically dynamic province of Guangdong (formerly known as Canton, where Shenzhen is located). The drive had many prongs—educational photo exhibitions, drug-burning ceremonies, amnesties for addicts, a drug rehabilitation drive combined with vigorous pursuit of criminals. By midyear, nearly 5,000 suspects had been arrested and over 300 kilos of narcotics seized. On a single day in May, fifty-one convicts, mostly drug traffickers, were executed. Operation Strike Hard, launched in 1996, has also proved effective, but the pro forma trials and rapid executions are disturbing, to say the least, to those with a respect for human rights and due process.

China's response was violent, but so are many of the criminals. Ngai Ngan Pun, a lecturer at the Chinese University of Hong Kong and an expert on crime, has said the ranks of Chinese organized crime were filled with people who had acquired a taste for violence during the Cultural Revolution but could find no place for themselves in the China of Deng Xiaoping. "In the 1980s, society was opening up and getting more competitive. These former Red Guards didn't have any formal education. They had no skills, no knowledge," he observed.

China's emerging middle class wants to feel that its property and personal safety are protected from crime. That is a service only government can provide and is part of the Communist Party's mandate for stability. The communists, serious about maintaining power, are in favor of vigorously prosecuting crime because that bolsters the party's otherwise shaky legitimacy. But tens of thousands of party members and government officials, who are perfectly aware that they live in a valueless society where only power and wealth matter, incline toward the money. Many can be bought, though for some of them large sums are required. Active triads and corrupt government are not ideal for stability.

Here, China and Russia share a similar problem—flight of domestic capital scaring off foreign investment. Foreign investment remains low in Russia, which during the early 1990s received less than one percent of the world's total capital investment. By contrast, China is well capitalized, with its annual gross domestic product more than four times the size of Russia's and valued by the World Bank at almost $3 trillion. But Chinese prosperity could change precipitously if a growing proportion of its own capital, the smart money, continues to flee the country and place its true vote of confidence, its deposits, anywhere but home.

Western law-enforcement officials claim that corrupt Chinese officials and businessmen as well as outright criminals are known to be depositing substantial sums in Caribbean banks. The money comes from two major, and competing, components of Chinese society. First, there is the Beijing money, funds siphoned out of government accounts or bribes involving Communist Party officials. This is their nest egg or rainy day fund, to provide for their families should power ever slip from their fingers. The second type of money is "hot money" out of southern China, generated through capitalist activity by entrepreneurs who want their capital to be in countries where it cannot be touched by Chinese bureaucrats.

If such people—who are on the inside and presumably in the know—are siphoning off large amounts of capital at the present time when the situation in China is still relatively calm, one can only imagine the capital flight that would ensue upon the first signs of genuine social disorder. When the peso fell in Mexico in late 1994, we saw how quickly large investors could move money out of a country. In China, the sudden sucking sound of money leaving in the wake of political instability could lead to severe recession, stagnation, even partial collapse. Ideal conditions for a "cult of personality leader." And "cult of personality leaders" are rarely great friends of the United States.

So China poses a challenge whether it succeeds or fails. We can hardly applaud a China that is adept at combining crime, capitalism, and communism. But we can hardly wish for one reduced to economic anarchy by metastasizing corruption.

The Nuclear Black Market

THE BLUR BETWEEN TRADE, criminal activity, and government is nowhere more dangerous to the national security interests of the United States than in the sale of nuclear weapons. If Libya, Iran, Iraq, or North Korea crashes the nuclear club in coming years, it will be because the Chinese government has sold the country the components, materials, and/or expertise to construct nuclear and/or chemical weapons of mass destruction. Political consider-ations appear not to be paramount here. Obviously, the Chinese will not sell nuclear materials or weapons to neighboring coun-tries with which they have hostile relations. But other than that, they seem to have few compunctions as to the buyer's poli-tics. Nuclear weaponry turns out to be just another modern com-modity.

In early 1996, then U.S. secretary of state Warren Chris-topher and his Chinese counterpart, Qian Qichen, held a series of meetings in an attempt to halt the downward spiral of Sino-American relations. Apart from intellectual property rights (IPR) violations, market access, human rights, and the mounting ten-sion over Taiwan, Chinese transfers of technology—in particular ring magnets—to assist Pakistan's nuclear program were a prin-cipal concern. The United States is considering imposing sanc-tions on the specific companies involved in the exports of the technology or barring financing by the U.S. Export-Import Bank of some $800 million worth of nuclear power deals in China.

Triads and Tongs

CHINESE CRIMINAL ORGANIZATIONS are usually known as triads. In the United States, another term is also loosely used—tongs. In fact, most U.S. tongs are legitimate business associations (the word in Cantonese means "meeting hall"), though some have been corrupted. And to complicate matters, some of the triads have modeled the structure of their organizations on that of the tongs. The typical triad is run by a "Dragonhead" and adminis-tered by a "White Paper Fan"; recruitment is carried out by an "Incense Master," with liaison performed by "Straw Sandals" and enforcement by the "Red Poles." Regardless of name, Chinese transnational mobs are fast becoming major players in the new world criminal order.

In August 1992 the U.S. Senate heard testimony from a convicted Hong Kong drug trafficker who provided the first public glimpse inside the secretive triads, hierarchical criminal corporations that evolved out of Chinese monasticism and have been operating among the mainland Chinese since the Ch'ing dynasty in the seventeenth century. The trafficker, identified only as Mr. Ma, joined the triad known as the 14K, which counts almost 20,000 members worldwide, at the age of fourteen in an initiation rite that included the drawing of blood. In what is a fairly common pattern, he later became a member of the Hong Kong police force, where he ran protection rackets; he then left the police force to run prostitution and loan-sharking rings. Eventually, he used a network of corrupt Nicaraguan diplomats to move narcotics into the United States, building a smuggling system that included access to shipping companies that would take heroin on consignment, hiding it in containers bound for New York.

Mr. Ma's opportunities were limited by the fact that Hong Kong is, after all, only a small city-state. Some of his colleagues have been more ambitious, moving operations to the mainland with its 1.3 billion potential customers. Already, the triads have set up front companies and restaurants in Guangdong Province as covers for prostitution, gambling, and extortion rackets; produced in China and exported more than 4 million metric tons of methamphetamines (speed) over the past three years; and begun the systematic smuggling of hand grenades and Kalashnikov-type rifles out of China and to Hong Kong.

Organized global crime among the Chinese is not new— its historical roots run deep, and its presence has been observed in Chinatowns from Kuala Lumpur to San Francisco to Cape Town for over a century. The triads began in mainland China as a form of self-protection against corrupt rulers, with adherents taking vows of secrecy, order, and loyalty that have changed little in four hundred years.

Today some fifty triads based in Taiwan and Hong Kong alone engage exclusively in criminal activities, including gambling, extortion, prostitution, loan-sharking, alien smuggling, and infiltrating legitimate businesses. Fueled by the money created by China's new entrepreneurs, they are expanding into real estate, too. Today, among other properties, they own a significant interest in the Fujian international airport (what could drug traffickers desire more than an airport of their own?) and the whole of Hong Kong's so-called forbidden city, soon to be absorbed by the mainland regime.

Traditionally, among the diaspora Chinese, a variety of organizations—everything from highly structured triads to loosely affiliated gangs—have preyed only on their fellow Chinese, backed up by the muscle of Chinese street gangs that usually sport poetic names like Ghost Shadows and Flying Dragons. But today they are expanding their turf, as demonstrated by their takeover of the American heroin market, a partnership involving a tong, a triad, and, until recently, a Chinese warlord in Myanmar (formerly Burma) once backed by the CIA.

The Chinese heroin trail begins, as it has for centuries, in the high jungle forests of backcountry Myanmar, where peasants harvest the sticky opium poppy for pennies a day. For more than thirty years that production was under the control of one man, Khun Sa, a former nationalist general who fled to Burma with remnants of Chiang Kai-shek's army after the communist revolution of 1949. Khun Sa got into the opium business under the watchful eye of the CIA, which wanted to keep his anti-communist army alive but couldn't provide the necessary funds. As the so-called prince of the Shan state, he ran a virtually independent fiefdom, enslaving the highland poppy farmers who harvest his product, and buying officials in Bangkok and Yangon (formerly Rangoon) to help him transport it.

In early 1996 the sixty-one-year-old Khun Sa, in poor health and shaken by the mutiny of his 15,000- to 20,000-man army, surrendered to authorities in exchange for amnesty. The mutiny was apparently sparked by the troops' increasing awareness that Khun Sa was more concerned with narcotics trafficking than with independence for the Shan state. Aggressive action by the ruling junta also played a role in his undoing. In recent years it had bought more than $1.2 billion worth of military equipment from China, including gunboats, air-to-surface missiles, helicopters, AK-47 rifles, and 107mm multiple-launch rocket systems.

The United States has offered a $2 million reward for information leading to Khun Sa's conviction in an American court, but the chances of his being extradited are essentially nil. His network had been the source of 60 percent of the heroin that reached the United States. He controlled about half of Myanmar's annual output of 2,000 tons of raw opium, which could be refined into 200 tons of pure heroin.

Originally claiming that he wished only the peace of semiretirement and intended to become a "chicken farmer," Khun Sa has won the right to operate a ruby mine and a bus company with a fleet of some three hundred vehicles, and has also received a license to import and export goods from China, among other countries. Observers of the scene remain skeptical about Khun Sa's newly found legitimacy. "Every business that Khun Sa is involved in is linked to heroin trafficking and money laundering," said an anti-narcotics agent based in northern Thailand. But the real question now is, did the control over the heroin trade simply shift from Khun Sa's hands to that of another group, just as the cocaine trade shifted from the Medellín cartel to the Cali cartel in Colombia? What we do know is that there is no shortage of heroin on the streets of America.

Guaranteed an increasing supply of new product from Khun Sa, and backed by the smuggling expertise of the triads, the Chinese tongs were able to enter the American heroin business with more than muscle alone. They cut prices relentlessly, forcing the Sicilians out of their traditional market. In the late 1980s, when it became clear that American heroin consumption was falling because middle-class users were squeamish about needles, the tongs introduced product differentiation as well, working with refugee chemists from the former French connection to develop "China White," a pure brand of heroin that could be smoked or snorted and has sent addiction rates soaring across our country, among people of all classes and races.

By the end of the 1980s, 60 percent of the heroin supply was under the control of the triads and tongs. As William Kleinknecht notes in his 1996 book, *The New Ethnic Mobs: The Changing Face of Organized Crime in America:* "In the new world of organized crime, no ethnic gangsters have a bigger future than the Chinese. While they may not yet approach the power of the Mafia in its heyday, Chinese crime groups are rapidly gaining power in cities around the country. In San Francisco, they are recognized by the FBI as the dominant organized crime group. They are second only to the Mafia in New York."

In fact, it's as difficult to gauge the true extent of Chinese crime in America as it is to measure corruption on the mainland. Officials from the Los Angeles Police Department's Asian Organized Crime Unit estimate that more than half of such crime goes unreported in Los Angeles County. Lack of respect for outside authority and fear of reprisal impose silence on many Chinese and other Asians.

The triads may well have the prosperous future Kleinknecht predicts for them because of their numerous inherent advantages. Unlike the Russians, they do not have to cultivate and construct a worldwide network. Forty million Chinese live outside mainland China in a diaspora even more far-flung than that of the Jews. Historically, the most widely distributed group are from the southern province of Fujian, which is situated directly across the Taiwan Straits from Taiwan. The Fujianese also predominate in the world of Chinese international crime partially because their language and its myriad dialects are impenetrable to outsiders, even Han Chinese. That makes infiltration of their groups and interception of their communications nearly impossible.

The Fujianese are closely allied with criminal organizations on Taiwan (many Taiwanese are originally from Fujian). It was in Taipei, the capital of Taiwan, that in March 1994 one of the largest single seizures of heroin was made—159 kilos with a value estimated at the time of $377.34 million. Some was for further export to the West and some for the island nation's estimated heroin addict population of around 60,000. The heroin had been refined in labs on the mainland. No doubt it had entered the country through Taiwan's main port, Kaohsiung. The world's third busiest port for container traffic after Hong Kong and Singapore, Kaohsiung is ideal for transshipment. According to the State Department's *International Narcotics Control Strategy Report* of March 1996: "Of the 2,904,360 shipping containers entering Keelung and Kaohsiung ports between January and November 1995, 24 percent were 'in transit' and, according to standard international practice, not normally subject to inspection by Taiwan customs. Customs inspects 15 percent of the remaining containers that are actually imported into Taiwan."

Heroin refined in labs closer to Guangdong Province

would have been transshipped through the harbor of Hong Kong with its traffic jams of ships. Unlike the narcotics trade of the Colombians, who prefer to control the entire cocaine business from cultivation to distribution, the Chinese heroin trade proceeds from one organization to another. For example, heroin arriving in Hong Kong would now be under the control of one of the city-state's seven major crime organizations that along with allied groups have a membership of between 50,000 and 80,000.

The number of containers passing through Taiwan's and Hong Kong's harbors makes it almost impossible to catch those that contain the heroin. And the money laundered by the triads slips by just as easily.

Piracy on the High Seas of High Tech

PRODUCTION, smuggling, and distribution of weapons net the triads in excess of $500 billion worldwide, according to the British national criminal intelligence office's latest estimates. Illegal arms sales also run into the billions each year. Corrupt members of the Chinese People's Liberation Army are selling immense stores of Chinese- and Soviet-manufactured weapons—Kalashnikovs, AK-47s, grenades, rocket launchers, etc.—to the triads, tongs, and Asian entrepreneurs who distribute them to criminals and terrorists worldwide. Chinese manufacturers were able to flood world markets with cheap Saturday night specials. The situation got so bad that the United States was forced to shut down the entire legal trade, which was threatening to swamp the United States with literally millions of low-cost, disposable, use-'em-once-and-forget-'em guns, as well as billions of rounds of ammunition. That market didn't disappear when President Clinton criminalized it. It just went underground, causing enormous headaches for U.S. federal gun inspectors. Thus, there was little surprise in the summer of 1996 when U.S. agents intercepted a major machine-gun smuggling ring in California and traced the weapons to businesses run by family members of some of China's most important leaders.

The switch to capitalism has created a nouveau riche class in China which, stimulated by a flood of advertising, naturally hankers for the better things in life. Each year transnational Chinese criminal organizations steal millions in yachts, luxury automobiles, and consumer goods, then smuggle them into China easily.

But the most costly thievery is not of tangible goods. That's what the Los Angeles Police Department's Asian Organized Crime Unit recently discovered. The unit consists of eight detectives, but their leader says they could use "a hundred." None of them speak Chinese or any other Asian language. It's not a question of prejudice but of policy. Detectives must have ten years' experience to work on that squad, and the pool of Asian-American detectives to draw on is simply still too thin. Nevertheless, the unit has had some outstanding successes. It cracked a major prostitution ring and broke a case involving 10,000 stolen credit-card numbers that represented a potential loss of $15 million to the industry. Most significant of all, the unit recovered more than $30 million in counterfeit computer software, CD-ROMs, and holograms. Subsequent investigation revealed an international network that led from the United States to Hong Kong and Taiwan before disappearing into mainland China.

Not only do transnational criminal organizations utilize modern technology, they also pirate and counterfeit it. The theft of intellectual property has already assumed such alarming proportions that it has become a sore spot in U.S.-Chinese relations. It alone amounts to as much as one third of all entertainment revenues on earth. Indeed, in 1995 and 1996, Hollywood's chief lobbyist, Jack Valenti, made repeated trips to China to demand a clampdown on the piracy. The entertainment industry losses go well beyond Hollywood, extending to the multibillion-dollar losses in the music business. Unchecked, this problem can only grow worse, as America's wealth tends to result more from the creation of software than from the production of hard goods. U.S. officials estimate that between twenty-nine and thirty-four pirate CD factories operate in China with a capacity of producing some 90 million discs a year. At just $10 a disc, this piracy alone represents some $900 million in state-tolerated, if not sponsored, piracy. Some discs are for domestic consumption, but the majority are exported, with Hong Kong serving as the major distribution point. Attempts by legitimate Western firms to establish joint ventures in China have met with official resistance —fear of "cultural pollution" serving as Beijing's rationale.

Enforcement of agreements on intellectual property rights has been lacking. Official Chinese cooperation on this problem has been intermittent and seems as a rule more designed to provide proof of compliance than to solve the actual problem itself. In April 1996, U.S. acting trade representative Charlene Barshefsky informed Chinese officials that the United States was considering imposing punitive tariffs equal to the roughly $2 billion in losses suffered by U.S. manufacturers of information and entertainment products.

In early June 1996, China's Most Favored Nation trading status was once again maintained, despite the intellectual property rights issue, which is creating more tensions between the United States and China than Chinese human rights abuses. Given China's role in the global marketplace as low-cost producer and the largest potential pool of consumers in the world, many trade experts question whether the United States even has the option anymore of restricting trade with China regardless of the circumstances. Such restrictions would have real consequences for American consumers and producers in the form of higher prices on imports and smaller market shares for key exports. This underscores the fact that, as a practical matter, the United States is helpless to do much unilaterally when it comes to illegal Chinese trading practices and commercial crime—or even human rights abuses.

Over the past decade Republican and Democratic presidents alike have reluctantly recognized the new reality of relations with China. We abhor human rights abuses but need multilateral actions to effectively have a significant impact on them.

Strategic Alliances

SINCE, AS WE HAVE SEEN, the triads have a host of advantages—a preexisting worldwide network, impenetrable languages and organizations, their own so-called underground banking system, a corrupt and compliant government at home—they have felt little need to operate outside their self-enclosed systems. However, in recent years, there have been indications that the triads are forging strategic alliances with similar organizations in Russia and Japan. Not only have the Chinese become the world leaders in trafficking in heroin and fake credit cards, they have also sealed alliances with the Japanese *yakuza*, the Russian Mafiya, and the Colombian cartels through their expatriate network.

As French journalist Roger Faligot has documented in his recent book on Chinese crime, *L'Empire invisible*, or *The Invisible Empire*, Chinese, Japanese, and Colombian criminals are working together in the cocaine trade in a variation on the old triangular opium trade between Europe, the Americas, and China: "The Colombian cartels produce the cocaine, the Chinese take it in exchange for heroin that can then be smuggled in the U.S. The triads bring cocaine to Japan and distribute it with the help of the Yakuzas. Then the Asian Mafiosi launder their drug money in Europe."

The triads have spun out extortion and loan-sharking operations to major British cities such as London, Manchester, and Glasgow; heroin trafficking to Rotterdam; prostitution, gambling, robbery, and contract murder to Germany; money laundering to Prague; weapons trafficking to Romania; and alien smuggling through Moscow.

In Japan, the triads are coordinating operations with the *yakuza*, which, composed of some 3,000 groups with over 85,000 members, is considered the largest criminal organization in the world. *Yakuza* means "nine-eight-three," the worst possible hand in a popular card game, and therefore signifies something like "born to lose." Japanese law enforcement prefers to refer to them as *boryokudan*, "the violent ones." Their tradition of violence goes back three hundred years to the samurai-type warriors during the civil war of the Edo period. Like the Chinese Red Guards who found themselves out of place in peacetime, these warriors turned to crime.

Of all criminal gangs, the *yakuza* are known to be the most frequent fliers—75 percent of *yakuza* members attempting to enter the United States were found to have multiple travel stamps on their passports. Not only are they busy spreading their narcotics distribution and money-laundering systems from Honolulu and Guam to the U.S. mainland, from Seattle to Boston, Los Angeles to New York, they are also networking with La Cosa Nostra and the Colombian cartels.

The *yakuza* have cooperated with the Taiwan triads, particularly the most powerful, the Bamboo Union, in setting up labs on Taiwan to produce methamphetamine. This is the drug of choice for Japanese addicts, whose population is estimated at between 400,000 and 600,000 (compared to the official estimates of China's entire drug addiction population of 380,000). Recently, aggressive police efforts on Taiwan have resulted in a shift of illicit amphetamine production to the mainland.

The Kidney Trade and China's Future

TRUE OR FALSE:

Government crackdowns on crime are good.

Lifesaving kidney transplant operations are good.

The answer is "true" except when China's ubiquitous corruption combines the two into a ghoulish and unholy business. Kidneys are for sale in the People's Republic of China at a price of around $30,000. Though the sale of organs is officially illegal, the kidney trade flourishes for the obvious reason that key sectors of the Chinese government—the party, the army, the justice system, the medical community—are all deeply and directly involved.

The business works like this: China tends to schedule executions around major holidays. For example, forty-four drug traffickers were executed in a one-week period at the end of August 1995. May Day is also popular. This is well known and allows prospective kidney recipients to make adequate arrangements beforehand. No announcements or advertisements are needed.

Executions are performed in the morning and the kidneys are then delivered within hours. One of five kidney recipients at the Organ Transplantation Research Center of the Tongji University of Medical Sciences in Wuhan City, Hubei Province, the largest facility of its sort in China, stated: "All five of us in this hospital had our kidney transplants done on the same day. . . . All came from young prisoners, all under 25 and very healthy. . . . They were executed at 11 a.m., and we had our operations at 2 p.m."

This man was lucky. Other patients have fallen even more seriously ill or died for a variety of reasons: poor tissue match between donor and recipient, AIDS, unpurified well water used during dialysis before the transplants were performed, poor post-operative care leading to high rates of infection, unqualified personnel involved in operations, low hygienic standards.

But most of the operations are reasonably successful and in any case it's a seller's market. Though conducted with a certain amount of discretion and stealth, this is hardly a clandestine operation—too many major social institutions are involved. Time is of the essence in kidney transplants, which means that efficient logistics must link all the players from execution cell to operating room. One hospital staff member at Number 7 People's Hospital in Zhengzhou, Henan Province, describes the procedure: "Everything is approved. We make arrangements with the executioners to shoot in the head so that the prisoner dies very quickly, instantly, and the survival rate of organs is considerably higher than from shooting through the heart. . . . We drive the surgical van directly to the execution site. . . . As soon as the prisoner is executed . . . and upon completion of necessary procedures by the police and the court, the body is ours. . . . We buy the whole body. . . . From a legal point of view, once a prisoner has been shot, he no longer exists as a human being."

The ideal donor is young and healthy. But the dead by definition cannot be particularly healthy and therefore the most important people—that is, high party officials—receive kidneys from prisoners *before* they are executed. A surgeon who had defected from China to Hong Kong told the Chinese-American dissident Harry Wu: "I was ordered to take both kidneys from an anesthetized prisoner. The organs were taken away by military helicopter. I can only assume it was for a high-ranking [Communist] Party member." Membership does have its privileges.

The harvest of organs following the May Day executions in 1995 had some disturbing political ramifications as far away as Hong Kong. The work of a popular cartoonist, Lily Wong, suddenly disappeared from its usual space at the bottom of page 2 in the *South China Morning Post.* Though the paper's executive editor insisted the cartoon was dropped for purely economic reasons, no one was taken in. Lily Wong just happened to be doing a series of cartoons satirizing the kidney trade when she suffered severance. In a recent cartoon, one guard says to another: "Don't beat the prisoners. Those kidneys are worth $30,000 each." But even though the price was quoted correctly, the Chinese government no doubt put pressure on the paper's board. Criminals are notoriously touchy about their honor.

The kidney trade is more symbolic than endemic. It is estimated that some 10,000 kidney transplants have been performed in China in the last several years and that 90 percent of the "donors" were prisoners. Viewed strictly in financial terms, this is not a major enterprise compared with, say, the drug trade —10,000 transplants at a rough price of $30,000 each amounts to $300 million over a period of several years. The human horror is, of course, incalculable, especially for those whose kidneys were removed while they were still alive and who were then brought out of anesthesia to be executed. Though a good many of these people may have been criminals by an ordinarily accepted international understanding of the word, they hardly deserved such treatment. Worse, some percentage of these people may well have been guilty of crimes that would not merit the death penalty in most countries—cases involving more than fifty grams (an ounce and a half) of heroin are capital crimes in China. And if any of those executed were simply human rights activists struggling for a better China, the horror is too great to even be imagined.

What counts about the kidney trade is not its scope but the scale of the collusion. The cooperation of the government, the army, and the legal and medical systems diffuses the focus of corruption that results when values have crashed and everything is for sale. That diffused focus makes Chinese crime hard to read.

China, of course, has its own share of the street crime that sours daily life in every city of the world. Much of it is committed by the "floating population," the millions of rural and industrial workers who have been shaken loose from the old "iron rice bowl" security of precapitalist China and who, infected by the get-rich-quick mentality of the times, aren't averse to simply taking what they want. And China has always had its traditional criminal organizations, the triads (so called in English because their Chinese symbol includes a triangle). Because of the 40 million Chinese dispersed worldwide, the triads had globalized centuries before the word even existed. The triads on the mainland, Hong Kong, and Taiwan, combined or combinable with the Chinese underworld in hundreds of major cities in dozens of countries, represent an unparalleled logistic and communication network, most of whose possibilities have as yet to be recognized.

But the pervasive corruption that hangs like a fog over China blurs all distinctions between business and crime, business and government. And that makes Chinese transnational crime harder to read and to penetrate. Though Russia may be in fairly desperate straits, the situation there is both dramatic and transparent. We can see what's going on. There is reasonably good government and law-enforcement agency cooperation. The FBI opened an office in Moscow in 1994, but it doesn't yet have one in Beijing, and the status of its operations in Hong Kong remains uncertain, as Hong Kong reverts to China. U.S.-Chinese tensions over human rights and trade continue to delay stronger bilateral law-enforcement contacts. The true extent of crime and corruption in China, like so many other things there in the days following the death of Deng Xiaoping, remains opaque, obscure.

Still, practically no one inside the country or out would argue that China is at a major threshold in its history, its future up for grabs. The economy is now more than half retooled to capitalism. The communists are still in power because they provide and guarantee the social stability that allows for rapid economic growth and because so far they have been willing to flex sufficient muscle to keep it. With the death of Paramount Leader Deng Xiaoping some change is inevitable. At the stroke of midnight on June 30, 1997, Hong Kong will revert to China, as will Macao in 1999. And that will leave only Taiwan. These can't be boring years.

The real question here is, in what way, if any, will China's drama of communism, capitalism, and crime impact on our national security?

There is no democracy to be endangered in China as there is in Russia. What's at risk in China is stability, which the Chinese leadership values more highly than unfamiliar and unpredictable freedom, especially when they see what freedom has wrought in their analogous neighbor, the former USSR. Stability is essential in a country of a billion-plus people riding the rapids of historical change. But crime is the enemy of both law and order. A China in disorder would be an international disruption of the first magnitude.

Nobody knows what China's future will bring. China is veiled by our ignorance, by its own preference for secrecy and discretion, and by its sheer numbers. There are too many people, too many factors in the equation for anyone to fathom. China has to be a mystery even to itself.

And perhaps especially to the men in charge. On February 18, 1996, in the Great Hall of the People in Beijing, China's leaders celebrated the Lunar New Year by pledging to crack down on crime, uphold traditional communist values, and retake Taiwan. What they failed to notice is that crime is outrunning any crackdown, communist values are dead, and Taiwan—at least its triads along with those of Hong Kong—is preparing to retake the mainland.

4

Who Stole Colombia?

WHAT'S WRONG with this picture?

Itaqui Prison in the highlands of Bogotá, Colombia, 1993. Prison guards are demolishing a portion of one of the main concrete-block walls. In the background directing the action is Jorge Luis Ochoa, one of the kingpins of the Medellín drug cartel. Even though the hole they have made in the wall is ample enough for Ochoa to pass through without having to squeeze, he remains where he is, exhorting them to work harder and faster. Is it beneath the crime lord's dignity to even so much as brush up against a wall as he escapes, labor courtesy of Itaqui Prison?

Apparently so, for it is not until a six-foot-wide section of the wall has been removed that Ochoa deigns to stroll out past the sweating guards to freedom. But a minute later he is back, though no longer on foot. Mad about cars, he is now at the wheel of his favorite vehicle, from which he could not bear to be parted —a 1931 Model A Ford. As Ochoa zips around the yard, the guards begin rebuilding the wall. After all, this is a prison, and Ochoa is, for a time, a prisoner of the Colombian government.

When John J. Coleman, assistant administrator for operations of the U.S. Drug Enforcement Administration, related this tale to my subcommittee, he added with admirable understatement: ". . . as to whether or not he [Ochoa] runs or continues to run this organization from behind prison walls, I suspect that anyone who would have the ability to import an automobile and literally have the prison wall removed to do so would probably be able to conduct some form of business from inside."

The witnesses—both lawmen and outlaws—who testified at my hearings on international crime in April 1994 provided me with the material for an article outlining how Colombia had become a narcodemocracy, which I published that same month in the *Washington Post*. I explained how drug traffickers had purchased critical personnel in every key Colombian institution, provoking a firestorm of outraged denial from the Colombian government and press, as well as headlines on the *Wall Street Journal* editorial page condemning my "reckless lies." When I suggested that drug money had entered the campaign war chest of Colombian presidential candidate Ernesto Samper, the *Journal* editorialist stated flatly that it was impossible. So did Samper, who was elected Colombia's president a few weeks later.

Then in September the senior U.S. anti-drug agent in Colombia, Joe Toft, retiring after six years in Bogotá, left with a blast, warning that he couldn't think of a single institution in Colombia that hadn't been penetrated by the traffickers. Toft said he had no doubt that cocaine kingpins had paid hefty sums to the campaign of President Samper. He also charged that the previous president, César Gavíria, now the head of the Organization of American States, had been aware of and done nothing to stop senior cartel figures from trafficking cocaine and ordering murders from their prison cells. An outraged Colombia demanded an apology from the U.S. State Department, and got it. Responding to the charges leveled against him, Gavíria said that his government, with the support of the United States and the international community, not only dismantled the Medellín cartel but also successfully apprehended Orjuela Caballero (one of the top drug dealers on the DEA's most wanted list) and Guillermo Pallomari (the so-called treasurer of the Cali cartel).

Soon thereafter, the United States publicly acknowledged what it had already told Samper—that his campaign had indeed taken drug money and become, in effect, a partner in crime with the cartels. The State Department recommended that Colombia be cut off from multilateral lending programs, "decertified" by President Clinton, for failing to cooperate with the United States in the war against drugs.

Meanwhile, the Cali cartel continues to buy up entire sectors of the Colombian economy, working to achieve a dominance over the government that will ensure them safe harbor forever.

Criminalization of an entire country is still only a threat in Russia and China; in Colombia, home of the world's most powerful global criminals, it is a daily reality.

Drugs have made Colombia rich; the nation is awash in profits earned by the export of cocaine to the United States and the rest of the world. But the country has been all but stolen from its people, virtually taken over by the drug cartels. Many legitimate businesses have been pushed out of the economy; businesspeople, from corporate CEOs to shopkeepers, cannot always afford to care about whether their cash flow—or their financial backing—is dirty or clean. Legitimate agriculture has been pressured, too; coffee is less attractive to grow when coca is so much more profitable. A willing army of young Colombians enlist with the cartels, dreaming of easy money, while some young Colombians join the police, army, and customs department just to make money by cooperating with drug criminals.

Inside the Cartels

AUTOMOBILES FIGURED in the destiny of another Colombian criminal, Gabriel Taboada, who, at the time he testified before my subcommittee in April 1994, was serving a twelve-year sentence in the Metropolitan Correctional Center south of Miami for conspiracy to import cocaine. Two and a half years earlier Taboada had offered key testimony in a Miami court against Panama's General Manuel Noriega as well as a rare and detailed look inside the Medellín cartel's day-to-day operations. Taboada's criminal career began in the early '80s, when Colombia had imposed prohibitive duties on the import of foreign cars. But the drug dealers had a tremendous appetite for luxury cars and cost was not a consideration. Their tastes were also quite particular —one, as Taboada noted, absolutely had to have the same kind of Ferrari that Tom Selleck drove in *Magnum, P.I.*

Taboada's scheme was simple but effective. He bribed diplomats, who were exempt from paying duty, to import cars in their name. They were paid the value of the car at the time, usually ranging from $25,000 to $50,000. He submitted to my subcommittee a list of the diplomats involved; the makes, models, and colors of the cars; and the ultimate purchasers. Embassy representatives from Peru, Denmark, Ecuador, Chile, Iran, Venezuela, Honduras, and the former Soviet Union were all too willing to play Taboada's game. One of his biggest customers was Pablo Escobar, the violent chief of the Cali cartel, who bought four Mercedes and a Jeep Cherokee. Another was Fabio Ochoa, another leader of the Medellín cartel, who outdid Escobar, buying five Mercedes, two Chevrolet K-10s, a Chevrolet pickup, and a Chevrolet Blazer S-10.

His ability to satisfy the cartel leaders' rapacious passion for cars soon made Taboada a welcome figure behind the scenes in the Medellín and Cali cartels, though his ultimate allegiance was with the former. His firsthand view provided us with new insights into the cartels' operations and fleshed out a great deal of what we already knew or suspected.

Taboada was especially informative on the mechanisms of corruption and the Medellín's policy of outright assault on the elected government. He noted that "the only thing the Colombian drug traffickers were afraid of [was] extradition." We had observed that in 1990–91 the cartels had hired lawyers, lobbyists, and public relations experts in Colombia and in at least one case in the United States to cleverly frame the extradition issue as a matter of national sovereignty—Yanqui go home. Taboada had personally played a part in bribing senators. But the Medellín cartel was not about to place its trust solely in the powers of persuasion. It unleashed a wave of assassinations "to such an extent that the Government had to surrender . . . ," Taboada related. The combined efforts of corrupt journalists, lawyers, lobbyists, public relations people, and hit men impacted on the very core of Colombian democracy—the constitution; rewritten in 1991, it now includes a provision initiated by the narcotraffickers that prohibits the extradition of Colombian nationals, thereby making Colombia a safe haven for the drug lords.

In Taboada's account, Colombia is simply riddled with corruption. Not only do the drug lords contribute heavily to every presidential and senatorial candidate's war chest, they went as far as providing airplanes for one presidential candidate's campaign, even "painting them blue because the candidate was a conservative."

Far too many Colombian institutions have people on the take. The air force allows the use of their landing strips; air traffic controllers protect shipments and flight plans. The police, too, are cooperative. It turns out that many of their highly touted seizures of drugs were prearranged with the cartels. Later the drugs were either returned to their "rightful" owners or kept by the police as evidence for trials that were unlikely ever to be held.

How did all of this happen? In the late 1970s, U.S. drug agents found that major-league drug-trafficking organizations amounted to as few as six to eight people from "farm" to "arm." Major shipments were marked in tens of kilograms, not metric tons. Then, as former car thief Pablo Escobar and the Ochoa brothers perfected the cocaine trade out of their hometown of Medellín, demand prompted ever bigger shipments. Law enforcement responded, too, interdicting more shipments in larger quantities. Protecting the shipments became a priority for the traffickers, as did protecting themselves. They built their own armies and security systems, which soon became the equivalent of the national security services of most medium-sized countries. Like intelligence agencies, they compartmented their activities, paid for information, and placed spies in their opponents' forces, especially law enforcement. Like intelligence agencies, they got access to telephones, tapped trunk lines out of Colombia, and used special software to analyze who was calling the American Embassy and the Drug Enforcement Administration. Their experts wrote their own security manuals, marked "top secret" and numbered for control. Their tradecraft allowed them access to governments throughout Latin America. Their money allowed them to buy the services of lobbyists and lawyers in Colombia— and even in the U.S., as in the case of former senior U.S. Justice Department official Michael Abbell, in the United States.

But the head of the Medellín cartel, Pablo Escobar, went too far. His violent style became an embarrassment to both the government and the Cali cartel, which preferred a more low-key, high-tech method of operation. In 1993, while in prison and guarded by Colombian police, Escobar summoned two of his partners, Moncada and Galeano, to settle a dispute over a missing $20 million. Apparently, they failed to come to amicable terms, because while inside the prison walls Escobar killed them both, chopped up their bodies, and fed them to his dogs.

In December 1993, after a long hunt, Pablo Escobar was gunned down by the Colombian police. A victory for the often-maligned Colombian law enforcement? Not quite.

Escobar had made too many enemies. Some of them— members of the Cali cartel, police, and turncoat Medellín gang members—had even banded together into an organization called PEPES (People Persecuted by Pablo Escobar). Himself a former alternate member of Congress, Escobar had begun blackmailing the very politicians he had bribed, extorting sums determined by the information on their finances he had stored in his computerized records. He had alienated the public with his savageries— the slaughter of judges, journalists, and jurors. And, of course, the good, honest men and women of the Colombian police were always Escobar's enemies. But the real reason Escobar fell was because he had become an embarrassing, old-fashioned obstruction to the grand and modern vision of the Cali cartel.

Here I think it's worthwhile to quote from the actual hearings:

> SENATOR KERRY: Would the Government have been able to get Pablo Escobar without the help of the cartel?
> MR. TABOADA (as translated): It would have been impossible . . . because, as I said before, the degree of corruption is so great that on many occasions they were just on the verge of catching him, but the intelligence filtered out, and his partners had to be the ones to hunt him down so that he could finally and ultimately be caught.
> SENATOR KERRY: So it is absolutely accurate to say that the police and the cartel were partners in Escobar's death?
> MR. TABOADA (as translated): Absolutely certain.

The "Bootleggers of Cocaine"

THAT'S THE MYTH the Cali cartel operates on. The exact rationale runs as follows: Cocaine is only the booze of the '80s and '90s. In the United States, liquor was first available, then prohibited, and ultimately legalized again. In England and Europe, cocaine and opium could be bought over the counter until it was criminalized. If some Americans could go from bootlegging to legitimacy in the space of a generation, why should things be any different in South America than in North America? To suggest otherwise would be nothing less than cultural imperialism.

The Cali cartel had come to a series of important realizations. All the killing might have been necessary at one point, but it no longer was. And it was bad for their image, so important to every serious organization in the modern world. Besides, everything you needed could simply be bought. There was no need for the rough stuff and no future in it.

Seizure of all essential social institutions has twofold significance for the Cali cartel. It brings the state, their principal enemy, under their control. And it allows them entree to the political process so that their ultimate dream of "legitimate high station" can be realized. Escobar, with his blazing guns and bodies chopped up for the dogs, was an anachronism, an obstacle, and an embarrassment.

Cali is against the outright and entire criminalization of the government. The higher political ambitions of Cali could not be satisfied by an obviously tainted government that would enjoy little prestige in the world. But there's an even more practical reason—it isn't necessary. Cali's ideal, which the traffickers have themselves called narcodemocracy, requires only sufficient influence on the political process, the economy, and the legislative and legal systems. This goal, now realized, was explicitly articulated to me by someone in a position to know—a former cartel member. He said that the drug traffickers do not own everyone in the Colombian legislature or law enforcement. But, he explained, they do control just enough people in each organization to get Cali's job done. "We have the illusion of democracy, but the supercartel controls it."

Cali has chosen sleeker means to its ends. The arrest in late 1995 of Gilberto Mora Meza and a raid on the offices of cartel chief Gilberto Rodríguez Orejuela produced astounding revelations. Mora, who has been called a "true genius in matters of telephone tapping," had generously bribed dozens of telephone company officials and personnel in order to be able to eavesdrop at will on any phone conversation in the entire country. The Cali cartel had free access to the national police and Colombian security organizations and had tapped the telephone lines of the U.S. Embassy in Santa Fe de Bogotá. It was even monitoring conversations between the U.S. Drug Enforcement Administration chief in Colombia and senior Justice prosecutors in Washington. When those recordings were disclosed in Congress, the U.S. Department of State issued a strong protest. But in the meantime, the intelligent application of money and technology circumvented a lot of problems. The cartel had the information it needed and the police could remain pure as the driven snow.

The Cali cartel also likes to think of narcotics as simply one of the many businesses in which it is engaged. And indeed it is true that unlike Escobar and his thugs, the Cali people have a variety of commercial talents and are not criminals because they have no other options. The Rodríguez brothers, for example, operate a highly successful chain of pharmacies, of all things. And the Grajales family has extensive vineyards throughout Colombia, and ships wines and fruit pulp all around the world. But sometimes the family has a little trouble keeping its various businesses apart—the barrels of fruit pulp they sent to Europe turned out to contain some cocaine as well.

A further advantage of owning legitimate businesses is that they provide an excellent means of laundering money. Unlike governments around the world that are strapped for funds, the Cali cartel, like all transnational gangs worldwide, has more money than it knows what to do with. No U.S. government agency that I know of is in the position of being able to bury $150 million in the ground for lack of any other place to put it. The problem is always how to clean up that money so it can be put to use. As we shall see in some detail in Chapter 8, "Where the Dirty Money Washes Up," Colombia has any number of ingenious mechanisms that, combined with lax laws, qualify it as one of the twenty countries to receive the State Department's "high" rating as a center for money laundering.

Though in many ways the Cali cartel is like a modern corporation, its operational side is structured very differently. Relying on techniques provided to the Colombians by former Israeli intelligence personnel, the basic organization is the cell, which puts the cartel closer to the worlds of terrorism and espionage than to commerce. It is simply safer for members of the different cells to have minimum communication among themselves. In many cases they do not even know one another. For that reason, communication, when it does occur, must be especially secure. The cartel has made lavish allocations toward that end. Hiring Washington lawyers to research the regulations for wiretaps, it can estimate the amount of time any given telephone will be freely usable. It buys a dozen mobile and cellular phones from a Radio Shack, uses them a few days, then tosses them away and starts again. In addition to encrypted faxes, satellites, and beepers, its communication system in the United States includes hospital pay phones, which, for some reason, it considers less likely to be bugged.

Communications are the nervous system of distribution, and excellent communications are more essential than ever now that the Cali cartel has become bihemispheric and is shipping product as far away as St. Petersburg, Russia, where during the Soviet period you couldn't even get a Bible past customs.

Cali not only ensures the integrity of its worldwide distribution system, it also guarantees the quality of its product—in this case acting more like a corporation than a gang. If the cocaine is laboratory defective or not sufficiently pure, the product can be returned and the money will be cheerfully refunded or can be used as a credit against a future purchase.

Illegal distribution entails complex logistics and an array of vehicles. Cocaine is smuggled in everything from condoms that are swallowed by small-time couriers known as mules (if the condoms burst they can cause something worse than unwanted pregnancy or venereal disease—a prolonged, agonizing death) to stealth-like semi-submersibles that have been photographed by the DEA and are capable of transporting a few tons of cocaine over 1,000 miles and thus can enter any country, including the United States, without having to cross a port of entry. Cali has several of these.

In some ways, those submersibles are perfect symbols of the Cali cartel's approach. Unlike the dramatically violent Escobar, it stealthily smuggles its products and insinuates itself into "respectability." But the differences are ultimately illusory. The Cali cartel, like the Medellín, is an empire based on murder and the cocaine-induced destruction of the human spirit. The Cali cartel cannot coexist with a democratic government. Between them there can be no negotiations, for in the end, only one can survive.

Today and Tomorrow

COLOMBIA IS STILL the world's leading refiner and distributor of cocaine—its annual production of 80 metric tons, processed in a network of clandestine laboratories, accounts for three quarters of the drug available worldwide. But having concluded that it makes better business sense to control as much of the entire process as possible, the Cali cartel has recently branched out into cultivation. In 1995, Colombia surpassed Bolivia as a grower and is now second only to Peru in the cultivation of the "white poison of the Andes."

And the cartel is diversifying. In recent years Colombia has also become a player in the cultivation, production, and distribution of cannabis (marijuana) and opium (heroin). Though minuscule compared with Myanmar and Afghanistan, Colombia's production of heroin is definitely on the upswing and part of a systematic market penetration. Testifying before my subcommittee, investigative journalist and news analyst Paul F. Reid stated:

> The Colombian entry into heroin is as well planned as the Japanese entry into VCR technology fifteen years ago. The Colombians seem to be trying to carve a niche out

of the Nigerian-, Mexican-, and Far East–dominated U.S. market. To that end, the Colombians are giving away free samples, prevailing on couriers to take some heroin along with their cocaine, and, most important, producing more of their own. . . . DEA "signatures" on Colombian heroin show an average purity of 85 to 90 percent, three times the purity of Mexican- and Nigerian-imported heroin. Once a user tries this drug, he does not go back to the "low test" grade.

Cali, however, is cultivating less opium than originally estimated—some 5,400 acres as opposed to 49,400. Because they are brightly colored, poppies are also easier to locate and eradicate than the coca plant, which blends in with all other vegetation when viewed from the air. A great deal of Colombia's rural economy depends on the cultivation of the coca plant, and eradication actions must be based on a host of ecological and economic considerations.

In 1995 senior Cali syndicate members—the brothers Miguel and Gilberto Rodríguez Orejuela and José Santacruz Londoño—were arrested or surrendered. The conditions of their confinement can hardly be described as onerous. For example, on February 23, 1996, Gilberto Rodríguez Orejuela suffered what appeared to be a mild heart attack, a "reinfarction." Immediately upon receiving the news his wife entered the prison compound in a luxury car and was apparently waved on through. Shortly thereafter, a team of cardiologists arrived to perform tests. Apparently, it was no more than stress brought on by a difficult day—the prisoner was conferring with a "pool" of his lawyers when the incident occurred, after a morning meeting with Monsignor Pedro Rubiano, president of the Colombian Episcopal Conference.

In many cases, the crime lords have plea-bargained with the government, suffered no forfeiture of assets, and received lenient sentences, which they accepted as part of the cost of doing business. Some simply took it as a form of early retirement, though, as with many retirees, inaction proved irritating. Londoño, for example, though arrested with much fanfare, apparently bribed his way into escaping from La Picota Prison in January 1996. The prison was clearly corrupted. Around the time of Londoño's escape, authorities at this prison discovered that the Cali cartel had installed a sophisticated counterintelligence system within the prison itself, allowing jailed kingpins to communicate with their contacts outside. They also discovered that a few days before Londoño's escape, the security window in the interrogation room had been replaced by three pieces of glass held by eight screws that were easily removable.

It is Londoño who is believed to have ordered the assassination in March 1992 of Manuel de Dios, the editor of *El Diario La Prensa*, New York City's largest daily Spanish newspaper. Manuel de Dios, a naturalized American citizen, was gunned down in a Queens restaurant because of a series of crusading articles he had written about the effect of the Cali cartel on his community in Queens. In early 1994, Wilson Majia Velez was found guilty of the assassination and sentenced by a federal court in Brooklyn to life in prison without parole. But he was only the triggerman. As then DEA enforcement chief John J. Coleman testified to my subcommittee: ". . . an extensive investigation conducted by the New York police authorities and the DEA and the FBI uncovered links directly back to Cali and to Santacruz Londoño." But from the American point of view the exercise was academic because Colombia's new constitution prohibits extradition. In the end, Londoño received justice, after a fashion. After the United States complained about his escape, the Colombian military tracked him down and he died "resisting arrest"—a convenient solution to the problem of impunity, since dead men tell no tales.

Even those who do experience some difficulty in prison are able to improve their lot. For example, a notorious butcher named Ivan Ordinola, believed to be responsible for dozens of drug-related murders, in 1995 got himself transferred from a prison cell in Bogotá to one more to his liking in his hometown of Cali; the first twenty-three judges said no, so his lawyers simply approached a twenty-fourth, who, for some mysterious reason, agreed to the transfer. And, as we have seen, physical confinement presents the Cali chiefs with no great impediment in running their operations, a demanding job whose stress can best be relieved by easily available women or a spin around the prison yard in their vehicle of choice.

The Consequences of Corruption

THE NARCOTICS TRADE has cost the good people of Colombia and Colombian democracy itself dearly for many years, but in 1995 and 1996 that cost edged toward the prohibitive.

Colombia lost its certification as cooperating with the United States against drugs in 1996, when President Clinton determined that the leader of its drug-corrupted government was in league with the traffickers. Colombia will no longer qualify for credits from the Export-Import Bank or the Overseas Private Investment Corporation. This could affect up to $1 billion in Export-Import Bank commitments and $50 million in loans and $540 million in insurance from the Overseas Private Investment Corporation. In addition, the United States will vote against any loans sought by Colombia from such development banks as the International Monetary Fund and the Inter-American Development Bank. President Clinton can also apply trade sanctions that could close U.S. markets to coffee, flowers, and other such legitimate Colombian goods.

Decertification coincided with—and to a great extent was based on—the State Department's annual *International Narcotics Control Strategy Report*. Though acknowledging Colombia's successes in the "arrest or surrender of six of seven sought-after senior members of the Cali syndicate," the report found that the government of Colombia

did not make adequate progress in other areas. In 1995 it did not take effective actions to prosecute and sentence the incarcerated Cali leadership to prison terms commensurate with the gravity of their crimes and to obtain the forfeiture of all criminally-acquired assets. These criminals have continued to manage their crime empires while in jail, and their trafficking organizations have not been dismantled. . . . Money laundering, a natural corollary of the cocaine trade in Colombia, was not significantly disrupted in 1995. . . . Colombia lacks adequate legislation to enable it to seize and effect the forfeiture of the mammoth illegally-derived assets of narcotics traffickers. As long as traffickers are able to retain this wealth they will maintain the ability to corrupt the legitimate activities of Colombian society.

The decision to decertify, which bracketed Colombia with such unsavory nations as Afghanistan, Iran, Myanmar, Nigeria, and Syria, was a serious blow to the country's prestige and pride. Colombia's foreign minister, Rodrigo Pardo, declared: "We consider unacceptable this interference in our internal affairs." Pointing out that Colombia spent more than $900 million in 1995 fighting drugs in a war that has already cost the lives of more than five hundred security agents, Colombian president Samper asked, "not unreasonably," to use the words of an article in *The Economist*, how many more Colombians must die before "consumer countries assume their own quota of sacrifice." And President Clinton came in for some domestic criticism for a decision that aligned him with Senator Jesse Helms and failed to punish Mexico—a key link in the Colombian distribution network—for reasons that his critics contended had more to do with peso-propping economics and NAFTA-related politics than the war on drugs.

Does the discussion seem to have strayed from coca plantations and jungle labs to the halls of Congress and the White House? But that's precisely the point. Crime has not only become global, its effects also extend far beyond the parameters of law enforcement, creating international political issues while generating domestic political crises.

Though the evidence is that his campaign—and possibly some of his subsequent decisions as president—was directly affected by cartel money, such as his refusal to reconsider the issue of extradition to the United States, Samper has refused either to step down temporarily or to resign outright. This has led to a situation that the country's Nobel Prize novelist, Gabriel García Márquez, has termed a "moral catastrophe." On the other hand, that catastrophe has produced an odd unity among the most disparate elements of Colombian society. Conservative businessmen and radical students, generals and guerrillas, bishops and terrorists—very odd bedfellows indeed—have all called for Samper to step down. In late February 1996 a group of 148 prominent business figures urged the president to consider resignation, saying the country was adrift because "the directors of the Samper campaign have made public confessions, which clearly and unquestionably admit that a substantial amount of drug-related funds was used to finance the said campaign." Using less diplomatic language, the terrorist organization Movement for the Dignity of Colombia has issued a threat: "You, Mr. Samper, have to leave the presidency or you will witness, day after day, the fall of the country's important figures. . . . Your armored cars will be of no use to you when a thousand-kilogram mass, guided by one of our kamikazes, crashes into you." Leaders of the church backed by the president of the Bishops Conference and army have added their voices to the chorus, as have Colombian diplomats and generals who have retired in protest. To top it all off, in a fit of moral pique, the guerrilla group FARC (Revolutionary Armed Forces of Colombia) refuses even to negotiate with a government whose legitimacy has been so deeply compromised.

In the months that followed, more and more Colombian senior officials were indicted on drug corruption charges by Colombian prosecutors, or resigned from office, unwilling to serve the increasingly discredited President Samper. Those who had once supported Samper, like former Colombian president Alfonso López Michelsen and the influential Colombian newspaper *El Tiempo*, advised him to resign for the good of the country.

The United States intensified the pressure, revoking Samper's visa on the grounds that he aided and abetted the drug traffickers. So did the traffickers: A group calling themselves the Extraditables announced that they would wage a war on the Colombian state if it decided to reinstate the extradition of drug traffickers to the United States. At the same time Colombia's police director announced that President Samper had received anonymous death threats for agreeing to consider discussions regarding extradition.

As the situation deteriorates, Colombians like *El Tiempo* columnist Hernando Gómez Buendia have concluded that their government is "no longer viable," warning that "Colombia is crumbling on the inside and on the outside," with no one offering a plan or a solution to restore Colombian institutions to a state in which Colombians, let alone the rest of the world, can have faith in their integrity.

The real problem is that the crisis has both divided Colombian society and sapped it of energy, making it what one commentator has called a "society that is out of harmony with the survival instinct." In an article entitled "We Deserve Him," published in March 1996, also in *El Tiempo*, that commentator, Enrique Santos Calderón, goes on to say:

> What is truly serious and grievous is the collective weakness that all of this reflects: the lethargy of a society that does not react to the incredible succession of events that have produced the presidential crisis—a society that wavers between passive indignation and mere indifference and is hardly in a position to complain of the decay that is undermining it. . . . Nor does there appear to be any greater awareness of the serious damage that has already been done to our country. Even if Samper left office tomorrow . . . major damage has been done. The institution of the presidency . . . will hardly elicit the respect it formerly enjoyed. . . . Not to mention what has been done to Colombia's image abroad.

The verdict is damning and, unfortunately, accurate. Colombia's presidency has been travestied—in July 1996, Samper was refused an entry visa to the United States. The narcotraffickers have succeeded in shaming their nation before the international community.

The True Crime

IN THE DAYS OF OLD, highwaymen presented their victims with a stark but simple choice: Your money or your life. But, as we have seen time and again, contemporary criminal organizations threaten more than treasure and immediate personal safety: The institutions that undergird democratic societies are also under assault. Though this is nowhere more drastically vivid than in Colombia, it would be a serious error to think that such problems are extrinsic, confined to distant South American countries. The danger is as close to us as Colombian cocaine is on our streets. Or on the streets of St. Petersburg, where, as we have seen, a budding democracy is already blighted by crime. By its very extent and nature, organized criminal activity poses a threat to democracies at every stage of development, including those that are advanced and well rooted like Colombia's.

Or ours. America's complicity as consumers does nothing for the moral health of our republic. It weakens our immunity to corruption, as innumerable police bribery cases have painfully demonstrated. And having pointed out that Colombia is on the State Department's list of top twenty money-laundering countries, I would be unfair not to mention that the United States also belongs to that elite club.

Organized transnational crime threatens America's interests, well-being, and national security both from within and without. It can be an agent of disturbance on the international scene —by thwarting Russia's democracy or upsetting China's stability. For the time being, although it drains the lifeblood of our treasure, violates the integrity of our borders, and robs us of our precious confidence, the greater threat to us is external. American presidential candidates still spend party money or even their own, not the mob's. And John Gotti is not driving any Ferrari around the yard at his high-security facility in the United States under the tender ministrations of the U.S. Bureau of Prisons, which exercises its most dangerous offenders in the chain-link human equivalent of dog runs.

Democracy is rare and recent in human history; the world can ill afford to lose a single one. In Colombia, crime has killed democracy by turning it into a grotesque and humiliating parody of itself. That might not be immediately apparent to the eye— outwardly, societies that succumb to crime and corruption do not cease to function. Children go to school, the trains run on time, the mail is delivered. But such societies have lost everything that counts—the dignity that only liberty confers and the respect of other nations. Today's Colombia is a sad monument for those thousands who fought to keep it free and a warning to all who would stay free. Brave people fought against the narcoterrorists and continue to do so. They deserve greater international support in the struggle to hold on to their country.

5

Reengineering the Drug Trade

DRUGS ARE THE SINGLE best-selling product in the world today, netting by conservative estimates $420 billion a year or, more realistically, $1 trillion, approximately three fifths the size of the federal budget of the United States. And the numbers are growing. As the market expands, the drug trade is changing from top to bottom; power is being consolidated at each level, and marginal players are being forced out.

As we have seen, the more "corporate" Cali cartel replaced the crudely violent Medellín organization. The Chinese triads, utilizing their numerous advantages, have moved from the margins to become a major force, whereas a traditional organization like the American Mafia is, at least for now, somewhere between an anachronism and an endangered species. The American narcotics market is being infiltrated by criminal organizations based in countries as far away as Nigeria and as close by as Mexico.

Trafficking becomes ever more sophisticated. Cocaine is hidden in the walls and support beams of cargo containers, within bulk shipments of coffee, frozen inside vast quantities of blast-frozen shrimp to deter drug-sniffing dogs, and even moved in submarine-like semi-submersible ships to avoid detection by conventional radar and sonar. Cocaine arrives in consuming countries concealed in crates of beach towels, inside spools of industrial thread, inside cans of lard, sealed with quartz crystals, in drums of fruit pulp, in avocado paste, in fish meal, and inside condoms stuffed into the intestines of boa constrictors. One trafficker poured liquid cocaine into a shipment of live tropical fish, keeping the fish protected in an inner bag of water.

Drug traders see increased globalization as their greatest growth opportunity, much as Toshiba, Compaq, and Mercedes-Benz do. But their situation is fundamentally different. Global ambitions in legitimate trade lead to the peaceful and ethical conflict called free enterprise competition. Violence is avoided because the combatants are constrained, for what they believe is their own long-term benefit, by criminal and civil laws and by rules and regulations, such as GATT and NAFTA. But no such protective constraints inhibit the growth appetites of drug entrepreneurs. There are no laws, no rules, and no honor among the thieves, tempters, and corrupters.

Drugs are different from most legitimate products; they are all virtually equal in the eyes of the consumer. It's true that the Cali cartel developed crack cocaine as a kind of "low end" high for people too poor to buy $100-per-gram powder; it's also true that the Chinese triads successfully competed against the Sicilian Mafia by a trade (mal)practice that our Department of Commerce would call dumping. By and large, however, it is very hard for drug merchants to differentiate themselves in the marketplace, to win customer approval in a peaceful contest. So success depends on violence—a violence that has escalated as the industry shakeout has progressed.

The result has been ever-bloodier turf wars, market struggles that ignite every day all over this country. Jamaicans gun down Dominicans, Dominicans ambush African-Americans, a Cali cartel member tortures and kills the family of a Medellín rival in a basement in Queens, New York. If Thomas Hobbes was right that human beings once lived in a precivilized state where life was "solitary, poor, nasty, brutish, and short," then many millions of human beings are now living in that state once again—in the malignant economy of addictive drugs.

Drugs drive almost all of the street crime that so disturbs America today; more than two thirds of those arrested for serious offenses test positive for narcotics. Crack cocaine is responsible for much of the blood that runs red on American streets, for 350,000 addicted babies born each year, for the lost souls—babbling, deranged, often violent—who fill our mental hospitals, for the destruction of countless families and whole city neighborhoods. This is the cost that the newly reengineered global drug industry exacts from their final customers, but we all are its victims.

The Rise, Fall, and Resurgence of the American Mafia

THE MAFIA and law-enforcement agencies don't agree on much, but on one point they're in harmony: The mob is having a crisis of values. "People do whatever they feel like," says former Gambino-family underboss Aniello Dellacroce. "They don't train their people no more. There's no more—there's no more respect." Ronald Goldstock, director of the New York State Organized Crime Task Force, refers to second- and third-generation mafiosi disparagingly as "mob yuppies . . . They have the values of their contemporaries."

Omertà—the Mafia code of manly silence in the face of any danger—may seem outdated in a laptop world, but it wasn't only cultural change that eroded that time-honored institution of La Cosa Nostra. Tougher laws like the RICO (Racketeer Influenced and Corrupt Organizations) and CCE (Continuing Criminal Enterprise) statutes, coupled with stiffer sentencing policies, have taken their toll as well. It was significantly easier to be a "stand-up guy" when a mob soldier had to choose between a three-year sentence and certain disgrace, not to mention death. A fifteen- or twenty-year sentence tips the balance in favor of law enforcement. Salvatore "Sammy the Bull" Gravano, who admitted to participating in nineteen murders, was facing life in prison when he decided to provide the testimony that resulted in a life sentence instead for John Gotti, the head of the Gambino crime family, the last "boss of all bosses" (capo di tutti capi). The federal government currently has more than a hundred mafiosi in its witness protection program, whereas a decade ago the number was minuscule.

Changes in emigration and economic patterns have also

weakened the American Mafia. Between 1900 and 1909, 1.5 million Italian males under the age of forty-five came to this country; in the 1960s only some 60,000 arrived on these shores. Improved economic opportunities in Italy have constricted the flow, and the greater possibilities of legitimate upward mobility in this country have also tended to deplete the ranks of those entering organized crime as a means of livelihood. That alone, however, is not sufficient to account for the drop in membership in the five major New York crime families from 3,000 in the early 1970s to a current low of some 1,200.

Certain of the old-time American institutions traditionally corrupted by the mob, like the city machines that impacted such large cities as Chicago, New York, Philadelphia, and Boston, had essentially disappeared by the 1970s, though Chicago's did hold on for another decade. In addition, the mob has been squeezed out of some of its other favorite venues, the casinos of Las Vegas and the labor unions. Other reasons for the American Mafia's decline include the failure to adapt to the new realities of the late twentieth century—new products, new markets, new competition. Writing in *Trends in Organized Crime* on "The Decline of the American Mafia," criminologists Peter Reuter and David Ronfeldt remark:

> The Mafia has failed to maintain control of the New York heroin market and has been a marginal player in the cocaine business everywhere. . . . By the late 1980s, the traditional circuitous route for Southeast Asian heroin, through Sicily, southern Italy, or France, had primarily been replaced by direct importation, via the West Coast, by Chinese and Vietnamese entrepreneurs. The Mafia proved helpless to deal with any of these incursions on its traditional territories. . . . Chinese and Vietnamese importers have come to dominate the importation of drugs into New York and Los Angeles; they are sufficiently competent at these activities that the price of imported heroin has simply collapsed, from $2,000 per gram in 1980 to less than $500 per gram in 1992.

Has the Mafia, glamorized and mythologized in a hundred films, been reduced to no more than a semi-legitimate organization whose principal occupations are limited to decidedly unglamorous garbage collection, construction, trucking, and fish markets? Some citizens, commentators, and even law-enforcement agents have expressed a certain nostalgia for the old-fashioned honor of the mob—after all, a mob hit was always clean and precise. Innocent bystanders, not to mention children on their way to school or sitting on their front porch, did not have to fear a hail of bullets as they do today. If a rival mobster was killed in a barber chair, the barber himself would remain unscathed. Some experts have compared the Mafia to the old USSR—a single enemy, known, stable, and relatively predictable. Today, in both the political and criminal worlds, a crazy quilt of rivals in conflict diffuses focus, resources, and energies. In fact, this has proved something of a boon to a resurgent American Mafia. The influx of Russian, Chinese, Vietnamese, and South American criminals has taken some of the heat off La Cosa Nostra and given it a breathing space in which to regroup. One of the advantages organized crime shares with all types of organizations possessing a history and a structure is the ability to learn from mistakes and make the painful adaptation to new realities. John Gotti may have been the last of the old mafiosi—sleek, charismatic, extravagant—but it is far too early to count the American Mafia out.

The temporary weakening of its American brethren has caused Italian-based organized crime to become more active in its native country, especially but not exclusively on the coasts. Three Italian organized crime groups—La Cosa Nostra from Sicily, the Camorra from Naples, and 'Ndrangheta from Calabria—together are already earning an estimated $110 billion a year from cocaine and heroin trafficking in Argentina, Australia, Bolivia, Brazil, Canada, the Caribbean islands, Peru, Venezuela, and most of Western Europe. Together, they supply the know-how to ethnic-based criminal organizations in much of the rest of the world. While the Italians concentrate on acquiring and distributing the drugs, their accomplices provide security in the form of local muscle to ensure that the goods arrive without interference. To ensure protection at the highest levels, the Italians also focus on the politicians—buying numerous high-placed officials in Italy itself, as well as branching out to "support" politicians in other countries, like Brazil, Pakistan, Spain, and Turkey.

The principal Italian criminal organizations are all involved in drug trafficking (cocaine from South America, heroin from the Golden Triangle) and money laundering, though some have other specialties—loan-sharking, the infiltration of legitimate business, counterfeiting, extortion. The big players are the Sicilian Mafia, a.k.a. La Cosa Nostra, composed of some 180 families with 5,000 members, most of whom are in the vicinity of Palermo; the Camorra, 30 clans with nearly 6,000 members, centered in Naples and the Campania region; the 'Ndrangheta, 144 cells of around 5,300 members, spread throughout Calabria; and the Sacra Corona Unità (the "Sacred Crown"), established in the 1970s, 20 clans that operate out of Puglia with a force of 1,200 to 1,400.

Of these four organizations, the Camorra has proved the most enterprising and flexible, though the highly secretive and violent 'Ndrangheta runs a close second. The Camorra has restructured and reengineered in recent years as the profits from its investments in legitimate business have far exceeded the illicit gains that provided the initial basis for those investments. Barry A. K. Rider of the University of Cambridge in England, executive director of the Centre for International Documentation on Organised Crime, has written:

> Whilst the Mafia has tended to remain centered in Sicily, the Camorra families have tended to relocate their operations to reflect their business interests. Thus, major figures involved in Camorra operations have been identified in residence in the USA and a number of European cities. . . . The Camorra has shown a degree of sophistication that two decades ago would have been dismissed as fanciful. There is evidence that to facilitate its financial operations it has managed to successfully penetrate the Italian financial and banking community and it is, of course, known that the Banco Scilla was nothing more than a Camorra front.

A 1994 FBI report, *International Criminal Enterprises: Nature of the Threat*, states:

> Within the last two decades, the ICEs [Italian criminal enterprises] have evolved from regional criminal groups based in southern Italy into international syndicates with

global ambitions and capabilities. These groups cooperate with each other and with other international organized crime groups in the trafficking of drugs and other illicit activities. Their criminal influence extends beyond Italy into other parts of Europe, North America, South America and Australia . . . Italian organized crime, whether Sicilian Mafia, 'Ndrangheta, Camorra or Sacred Crown, has developed cooperative criminal networks amongst themselves and other organized crime groups, whether Asian, Colombian or Eurasian in origin, which supersede traditional law enforcement territorial boundaries.

Let us take a single example of the way in which the modern-minded Camorra has branched out internationally. An Italian law-enforcement operation code-named Vodka revealed the following in March 1995: The Camorra had linked up with Russian Mafiyas as partners. The Russians received counterfeit hundred-dollar bills, a Camorra specialty—one-dollar bills are bleached out, then reprinted as hundreds. The Russians circulate the bills through bases established in twenty-nine countries. According to the Rome Confcommercio report on Italian and Russian criminal activities, "today more dollars circulate in Russia and the Eastern European countries than in the United States." In exchange, the Italians received Russian currency, property in the former Soviet Union—possibly including a large bank in the Russian city of Yekaterinburg (formerly Sverdlovsk, the town where Boris Yeltsin rose to prominence when he was a member of the Communist Party)—as well as significant shipments of armaments, including rocket-propelled grenade launchers and anti-tank weapons. The Russians also provide the Camorra with large quantities of the synthetic narcotics that are now becoming a major industry in Russia. Not to be outdone by their Italian counterparts, the Russians have also invested heavily in Italian property, buying several hotels around Rimini on the Adriatic coast that are used to launder money, provide legitimate income, and house displaced émigrés who are then drawn into illicit activities.

Senate hearings in May 1996 revealed that, perhaps in an effort to modernize and rejuvenate, the American Mafia has struck similar alliances. In a now familiar scenario of a high-placed Mafia figure betraying *omertà* for a reduced sentence, Anthony "Gaspipe" Casso, fifty-six, the former acting boss of the

Lucchese crime family in New York, who had been on the run for nearly three years, was arrested by the FBI in January 1993; after agreeing to provide testimony for the government prosecution, he entered the witness protection program. What is not familiar, however, is the substance of Casso's testimony. Speaking on conditions of anonymity, a committee investigator said: "Casso will tell how the New York mobsters used their muscle to cash in on schemes and frauds that the Russians developed, especially gasoline tax frauds and gasoline bootlegging. . . . The Russians supplied the brains and the Mafia supplied the hit men." Further allegations include attempts to extort money from Russian players in the National Hockey League, among others, Alexander Mogilny, who, at the time, was with the Buffalo Sabres. This is one among several signs that the American Mafia has read the writing on the wall and begun to exploit the new realities of the times. It had better move fast, because the competition is leaner, meaner, and swifter of foot.

Other Players

NIGERIA

Everyone wants a piece of the multibillion-dollar American and European drug market. Some pursue it out of deliberate greed while others, like the Nigerians, enter the competition more as a result of circumstance. The collapse of oil prices in the 1980s had a devastating effect on the economy of Nigeria; by 1989 the World Bank for the first time classified Nigeria as a low-income country. According to a Brookings Institution study, *Global Habit: The Drug Problem in a Borderless World* by Paul Stares, published in book form in early 1996:

> The combination of worsening economic conditions and inadequate government services, especially in the already overcrowded cities, spawned a crime wave during the 1980s that eventually developed a drug component. Mean-

while, many Nigerian students who had gone abroad with the help of generous educational subsidies were suddenly stranded when their financial support was terminated as a result of cutbacks in government spending. Some of these initially turned to financial fraud, and later to international drug trafficking, to support themselves. By 1990, 26 percent of the heroin intercepted coming into the United States was credited to West African traffickers. With Lagos as the principal center of their operations, the Nigerian trafficking organizations have recruited hundreds of individual couriers to smuggle drugs, using the international airline network. By 1994 INTERPOL rated Nigerians as the third largest ethnic group engaged in drug smuggling.

With the exception of marijuana, most drugs have a high ratio of value to weight. Those with the greatest value—heroin, cocaine, and the synthetics—are almost odorless and are easily disguisable. The Nigerian smugglers tend to carry small amounts and to work in large numbers. The country is the most heavily populated in Africa, so finding replacements for arrested traffickers poses no problem. The pool of desperate young people willing to run the risk is very large. But the risks are high. In 1995 alone more than twenty-five Nigerians were publicly beheaded in Saudi Arabia for trafficking heroin. Saudi Arabia is a popular transshipment point for Nigerian couriers en route to Europe since it is relatively easy for Nigerians to obtain Saudi visas. Most of them are arrested at the airport. When Hamid Opoyaru, a counselor at the Nigerian Embassy in Riyadh, was asked whether his government had any intention of protesting the beheadings as barbaric, he replied laconically: "No, we just concede that that is the Saudi practice."

The shipping of heroin from Asia to the United States and Europe, as well as of South American cocaine to South Africa and Europe, has made Nigeria a significant player in the international drug trade. The country also makes the top twenty list of most important money-laundering countries in the world. Needless to say, with these levels of money, corruption is rampant. In 1996, President Clinton informed Nigeria that, as in the case of Colombia, the United States would vote to cut off lending to it by international organizations because of its failure to cooperate with the United States against drugs, a step required by Congress under laws governing U.S. foreign assistance.

And, like Colombia, Nigeria responded with a barrage of criticisms of the United States which, while substantively accurate ten years ago, were here perverted for purposes of self-justification. The special adviser to the head of state on drugs and financial crimes, Alhaji Adamu Muhammed, contrasted the two countries in a blast of indignation: ". . . if you compare the United States and Nigeria, who is the drug trafficker? Who is the drug manufacturer? Who is the drug consumer?

"If any drug trafficker is arrested in Nigeria, the maximum sentence is twenty-five calendar years, meaning he spends in prison, every single day of those twenty-five years. In the United States . . . they give him about five years, six years, and then out of the five, they give him two years' parole."

Were this accurate today, our sins still would not excuse theirs.

AFGHANISTAN AND PAKISTAN

World events are often inextricably linked with the growth of crime. Just as the collapse of oil prices stimulated a surge of criminal activity in Nigeria, the invasion of Afghanistan by the Soviet Union in 1979, coupled with Ayatollah Khomeini's crackdown on drugs in Iran, shifted the axis of the Afghani poppy trade. Pakistan became an important processing and transshipment point. And, in a now familiar pattern, the freedom fighters (mujahedin) increasingly viewed narcotics traffic as a source of income to purchase the weaponry required to defeat the Soviets, who far outgunned them. The governments of both Pakistan and the United States turned a blind eye to this trade. As Paul Stares writes: "Drug control evidently became subordinated to larger geostrategic goals."

After Myanmar, Afghanistan is the world's largest producer of opium. U.S. satellite surveys show a 33 percent increase in poppy cultivation in 1995 over the amounts produced in the previous two years. Some of that was lost to traffickers as a result of eradication programs in the area under effective government control, but most of that country, racked by civil war for the past eighteen years, is without even rudimentary law and order.

Though the poppy farmers of Afghanistan receive a pittance for their product compared to what others will garner down the line, survival itself impels them to grow what can be sold in a country where daily life is dangerous and anarchic, to say the least.

In the autumn of 1996, Taliban fighters, Islamic fundamentalists who had taken over Afghanistan's capital city of Kabul, executed the last Soviet-installed leader of the country and called for a return to Islamic purity and a repudiation of opium trafficking. But Western intelligence analysts immediately detected evidence that the public statements were a sham to mask continued smuggling by Taliban forces.

There is mounting evidence that Afghanistan is now seriously involved in processing raw opium into heroin. Though evidence remains sketchy, major shipments of precursor chemicals are reportedly entering Afghanistan through its borders with the former Soviet republics of Uzbekistan and Turkmenistan. According to the State Department's *International Narcotics Control Strategy Report* of March 1996: "Heroin base and morphine are smuggled out of Afghanistan and into the international market by sophisticated Pakistani trafficking organizations operating out of Quetta, Pakistan. These groups place orders with the Afghani processors and arrange for transshipment of the drugs. . . . Most Afghan opium is destined for processing into heroin in Turkey. The finished heroin is sold primarily in Europe, and to a lesser extent in the US."

Some of the drugs remain in Pakistan itself, which has 3 million addicts, half of whom are addicted to heroin. It is estimated that one in every twenty males over the age of fifteen is an addict, giving Pakistan the "most serious heroin abuse problem in the world," according to Giorgio Giacomelli, executive director of the UN International Drug Control Program. Most users smoke the drug, but the number of those injecting it with hypodermic needles has risen sharply in recent years.

According to Giacomelli, the drug trade now accounts for 5 percent of Pakistan's gross domestic product. Though it is only rated "medium high" as a center for money laundering, Pakistan now has a significant number of legitimate businesses taken over by organized crime. "Colombianization" is a danger, as Prime Minister Benazir Bhutto noted in 1994: "We do not want Pakistan to become a country of Latin America where terrorism is the order of the day and the drug mafia is given protection." At the moment Pakistan seems to be winning the war, with opium seizures up 1,385 percent in 1995 and an ambitious program created by the Narcotics Control Division which calls for eliminating opium production and making the country drug-free by the year 2000. But, as we have seen all too many times in our own country, stepped-up seizures and bravely named campaigns usually do little to slow the flow of drugs. The reason is simple: The narcotics trade is a global business and cannot be overcome by any country on its own. If there is a solution, it must be as concerted and international as the enemy's operations. No country is an island.

In September 1996, Prime Minister Bhutto suddenly raced in hysteria and tears to Karachi, a city overtaken by lawlessness where drug traffickers and terrorists compete for control with various factions of the Pakistani government. Her only brother, who had surrounded himself with his own private militia, had been killed in a shoot-out with local police, with each side claiming the other had shot first. In November, just a little more than a month after the death of her brother, Prime Minister Bhutto herself was forced out of office by Pakistan's president, who charged her and her husband with corruption, temporarily leaving no one even nominally in control in Pakistan. This is the kind of political vacuum made for exploitation by drug traffickers and terrorists as well.

MEXICO

Its 2,000-mile border with the United States affords Mexico a unique geographic advantage in the world of transnational crime. Easy proximity to the world's largest consumer of drugs is a market advantage that Mexican criminals have only just begun to fully exploit. In the American popular imagination, Mexico is viewed primarily as the source of large numbers of illegal aliens whose straining of the social services networks has now become a hot political issue nationwide. But as we shall see in Chapter 8, Mexico is also one of the principal conduits for the Chinese "human contraband" trade. One of the world's twenty most important money-laundering centers, Mexico is also now playing a burgeoning role in the cultivation and distribution of narcotics.

It may not be very long before Mexico's Gulf cartel is as familiar to us as the Medellín and the Cali cartels.

"Because the porous 2000-mile U.S./Mexico border and daunting volume of legitimate cross-border traffic provides near-limitless opportunities for smuggling activities and escape for fugitives, no country in the world poses a more immediate narcotics threat to the United States than Mexico," states the *International Narcotics Control Strategy Report* of March 1996. Somewhere between 50 and 70 percent of South American cocaine that enters the United States, as well as 80 percent of the foreign-grown marijuana consumed in this country, is funneled through Mexico. Each day five thousand trucks enter the United States from Mexico, but only two hundred are inspected. Mexican transnational criminal organizations have also branched out into opium poppy cultivation and heroin production, currently producing 20 to 30 percent of the heroin consumed in the United States. Mexican criminal organizations now dominate the manufacture, sale, and distribution of methamphetamine in the United States and have grabbed a significant piece of the market for designer drugs like Ecstasy, popular in the club world of American cities, and illegal steroids.

The Mexican government is aware of this problem and making strenuous efforts to combat it. President Ernesto Zedillo has declared drug trafficking "Mexico's number one security threat." In 1995, Mexican authorities showed considerable progress in the number of arrests made, labs destroyed, and crops eradicated. Many of the key figures were arrested, including José Adolfo de la Garz-Robles, believed by U.S. officials to be the main contact between the Gulf cartel and the Colombians, and José Luis Sosa Mayorga of the Gulf cartel, who is suspected of coordinating the flights between Colombia and Mexico. Nevertheless, narcotics continued to flow into Mexico from South America, in part because traffickers have at their disposal speedier and more sophisticated aircraft that are able to carry multiton loads and elude Mexico's monitoring systems and pursuit planes. But there is another reason, less technological, more human, all too human.

The frightening situation in Mexico at the beginning of the Zedillo administration in late 1994 exemplifies the potential impact of corruption on the political process. First, drug cartels and corruption were linked to three high-profile assassinations prior to the last Mexican election: of Cardinal Juan Jesús Posadas Ocampo at the Guadalajara airport; José Francisco Ruiz Massieu, secretary-general of the ruling Institutional Revolutionary Party (PRI), outside a Mexico City hotel; and PRI presidential candidate Luis Donaldo Colosio at a Tijuana campaign rally. Then, amid a massive financial crisis linked in part to political instability, senior officials and relatives of senior officials from the previous administration were charged with having colluded in cover-ups of assassinations, perhaps in partnership with drug barons. One could not get much closer to the heart of the previous Mexican administration. Those arrested included both the elder brother of the former president, Carlos Salinas, for allegedly masterminding the Massieu murder; and Mario Ruiz Massieu, the former Mexican deputy attorney general, who investigated his brother's murder, charged with taking millions of dollars in bribes from the Gulf cartel during his tenure as Mexico's senior narcotics official. Editorial writers referred to it as "Mexico's Greek tragedy," noting that amid "venality and kin murder, the triumvirate of corruption, modernizing, and drugs now rules."

Eduardo Valle, former drug adviser to the Mexican attorney general, now living in exile in Washington, charges that "narco-power is becoming a state within a state in Mexico." Valle contends that traffickers cannot stop the government from making decisions, but can stop it from implementing them, with the result that regardless of who is in power, the traffickers control what will enable them to continue to flourish.

While the Zedillo administration professes its intention of cleaning up the mess, professionalizing the police, and ending the impunity that had come to undermine respect for political institutions in Mexico, additional scandals have surfaced. In Mexico City, the transport chief was found dead of gunshot wounds the same day authorities revealed an alleged $8 million fraud involving the bankrupt municipal bus system and its union. In May of that year the son of one of the PRI's most important political figures, Carlos Hank González, was arrested on smuggling charges. Carlos Hank is himself rumored to be a billionaire whose fortune was made, according to Mexican press allegations, through manipulation of privatization and government contracts. A few days later the former state attorney general responsible for investigating Cardinal Ocampo's murder was assassinated in Guadalajara in a killing that appeared to be the work of drug traffickers. The official, Leobardo Larios, had concluded that the cardinal's death was a matter of his being in the wrong place at the wrong time during a drug shoot-out, despite the fact that the cardinal was shot fourteen times at point-blank range. Recently, Mexican officials have suggested that the cardinal's shooting was deliberate, and questions have been raised about ties between state law-enforcement officials connected to the case and the traffickers.

In late July 1996, a senior Mexican drug official called the Mexican drug war a "joke." Ricardo Cordero Ontiveros, former head of the National Institute for Drug Combat branch in the border city of Tijuana, told reporters of a corrupt partnership between senior Mexican law-enforcement officials and Mexican drug traffickers to secure their release should they be captured by lower-level drug agents. When he complained to the Mexican attorney general, he said the attorney general told him that people would pay $3 million to have his job. Utterly disgusted, Cordero resigned. Ironically, Cordero himself was arrested by the Mexican government soon after going public with his charges.

The farcical elements of Mexican law enforcement too often veer, in practical terms, into the tragic. In the fall of 1996, one after another, the most respected prosecutors and investigators of major drug crime in northern Mexico were murdered in a series of assassinations undertaken by hit men for the major cartels.

The killings continued into early 1997, when gunmen in Tijuana assassinated a senior prosecutor investigating the previous drug-related killings; he was the eighth senior Mexican official working on drug cases in Tijuana to be murdered. The murders testified to the fact that some in the Zedillo administration were serious in going after the traffickers and their power. The murders, none of which have been or are likely to be solved, also highlighted clearly the fate of those who challenged the drug lords and their ties to the Mexican government, and the impunity with which the criminals could retaliate.

All of this underscores the impact on Mexico, over time, of corruption linked to crime. Examples of how corruption and crime are linked in Mexico have unfortunately been all too frequent and obvious. For example, in August 1994 in Sombrerete,

Mexican federal police officers seized 10 tons of cocaine from Colombia, which became only 2.5 tons when it was turned over to the government. In the days that followed, U.S. drug agents observed quantities of the cocaine moving from Mexico into the United States.

On the day of his inauguration, December 1, 1994, President Zedillo expressed to Attorney General Janet Reno his intention to reform the administration of law in Mexico by professionalizing law-enforcement agencies and combating official corruption. Early in his presidency, President Zedillo proposed a package of judicial reforms that both houses of the Mexican Congress quickly approved by overwhelming majorities. Among the most important of the reforms would be establishing a greater degree of separation of powers, creating the kind of checks and balances more likely to discourage corruption than the present system. At bottom, as analysts at the Rand Corporation concluded in 1992, "the Mexican drug problem . . . is essentially an integrity issue."

Will the Zedillo government respond to the warnings given by former Mexican officials like Valle and Cordero? Can Mexico transform its law-enforcement system into something that has enough integrity to combat the wealth of the traffickers? The consolidation of Mexico into a modern, free-market economy and democracy requires positive answers, even as the free market has made it harder to achieve success.

Significantly, Mexico's decision to move away from state socialism to privatization during the Salinas administration exacerbated the situation.

The transformation of Mexico's political and economic system over the last few years has weakened the old system of centralized control by the Institutional Revolutionary Party that has run Mexico for most of this century. As the PRI fragments into a technocrat wing, headed by President Zedillo, that controls little, and a dinosaur wing, typified by Carlos Hank González, that is increasingly corrupt and ossified, Mexico starts to reflect Yeats's words, "Things fall apart; the center cannot hold." The traffickers fill the vacuum, more and more prosecutors are murdered, and impunity threatens the foundation of democracy.

In 1996, President Clinton was faced with an ugly choice.

He had to tell the U.S. Congress whether or not Mexico was fully cooperating with us against drugs. If he acknowledged the truth, that Mexico could not cooperate effectively against narcotics because the institutions that President Zedillo presided over were collapsing, he risked weakening Zedillo and reform efforts still further. If he avoided the truth, too many people on both sides of the border could continue to pretend that nothing was seriously wrong. Receiving conflicting advice from senior advisers, the President told Congress that Mexico was fully cooperating. He came under a storm of criticism. Senators from Republican Alfonse D'Amato of New York to Democrat Dianne Feinstein of California charged that the President did not care about fighting narcotics but only about protecting the $12.5 billion in loans to Mexico that his Treasury secretary had arranged to shore up the Mexican economy after the collapse of the peso in late 1994. By early 1997, the situation in Mexico continued to worsen—more killings, more high-level corruption, even greater threats of instability. For this situation, both Mexico and the U.S. were at fault. Neither country had faced the implications of moving ahead with privatization and free trade without simultaneously moving ahead with the necessary political and law-enforcement reforms.

In truth, loans or no loans, the policy dilemma remains acute: How does a country like Mexico, whose law-enforcement institutions have been overwhelmed by drug-related corruption, outgunned by drug-trafficking hit men, and undermined by drug-infiltrated political parties, protect its own people from the traffickers, never mind being a reliable partner against drugs for the United States?

The future of Mexico is as uncertain as that of any country of its size and importance anywhere in the world. The greatest threat to that future, by the estimation of its senior officials, is nothing less and nothing more than the cocaine trade.

A Day in the Life

MAJOR NARCOTICS BUSTS still occasionally make the national news, and the numbingly familiar random extinction of young lives is a staple of the local news. But whether ballyhooed or underplayed, the business of narcotics continues day and night around the globe. One group that tracks the trade and its consequences is the U.S. government's FBIS (Foreign Broadcast Information Service), which issues a daily report entitled simply *Narcotics* that typically runs close to a hundred pages. Choosing one issue, that of April 5, 1996, we learn the following:

• Major seizures of narcotics occurred all over the planet. The Czech Republic reported its largest seizure ever of marijuana (6 tons), packed in containers with cotton and en route to Belgium. The French broke up a drug-trafficking ring in the Pyrenees. Iran impounded 235 kilos of opium, and security services in Morocco confiscated 62 kilos of cocaine from a ship, the *Astrakhan*, which, according to the Lloyds register, should have been flying the Russian flag instead of the Cypriot. The ship's entire crew of twenty-four and the captain are Russian nationals. The cocaine was concealed in a shipment of coffee beans from Brazil and was due to be unloaded at the Italian port of Genoa. This was yet another instance of increased cooperation between the mafias of Russia and Italy.

On that same day, significant seizures also took place in Argentina, Bolivia, Chile, Paraguay, and Peru. In China, the Guangxi border police reported record seizures, and Singapore reported the breaking of a major heroin syndicate. Israeli police intercepted a record amount of South American cocaine (43 kilograms of pure cocaine valued at $3 million) in the port of Haifa en route from Holland. Both heartening and disheartening, the list goes on. It is heartening because it demonstrates the effectiveness of country-by-country efforts to fight drug trafficking and disheartening because we know that for the traffickers the amounts seized are viewed merely as the cost of doing business, and for every kilo seized, 10 kilos get through.

• Well armed and vicious, drug traffickers do not meekly surrender to law-enforcement agents. Police came under fire in Upper Egypt. And in Baja California, Mexican traffickers opened fire on a Mexican Navy helicopter sent to intercept. The Mexican Navy, which has been pressed into service in the drug war, performed well that day, sinking one of the two smuggling vessels and arresting four traffickers.

• The corruption that, like money laundering, always accompanies drug trafficking, also made news that day. The crisis around Colombia's president, Ernesto Samper, dragged on. In Bolivia, a judge who hears narcotics cases was videotaped and arrested "red-handed" while accepting a bribe.

But corruption is hardly limited to presidents and judges. In Russia, where drug seizures have jumped from 50 kilograms in 1992 to 6 tons in 1995, the temptations of trafficking lure not only the young, wild, and violent, but also the old and poor, dispossessed by the turmoil of that society's transition from communism to capitalism. In the Transcarpathian region in southwestern Russia, one out of every ten drug pushers or producers is a retired person living on a pension. Not only is the typical pension too meager to live on, the state has not even paid most pensioners since the fall of 1995. So Russia has seen the birth of a new phenomenon that the newspapers have already dubbed "narcogrannies" and "narcograndpas."

• Corruption extends even to the animal kingdom. A report from the former Soviet republic of Azerbaijan, which borders on Iran, quotes Mubariz Guseynov, chief of the Main Administration for the Fight Against Drug Addiction and Narcobusiness of the Azeri Ministry of Internal Affairs: ". . . specially trained animals [camels] . . . would be loaded with dozens of kilograms of opium in Afghanistan, and then the animals, by themselves without any guides, would follow deserted mountain trails and arrive at the designated point." When "arrested," the camels are routinely destroyed by Iranian police.

Tomorrow and Tomorrow

PREDICTING THE FUTURE is always a tricky business and never more so than in a period of high-velocity change like our own. It does seem quite likely, however, that globalized crime is here to stay and, unless combated by new, forceful, and concerted efforts, will only pose an ever greater threat to stability and liberty around the world.

The past may well prove a reasonably reliable guide to the future as far as the drug trade is concerned. We can expect new drugs targeted for new markets. Here crack can serve as a paradigm. Named for the crackling sound the cocaine crystals make as they burn, crack was unknown in the early '80s but had become the scourge of American cities by the end of the decade. "One day nobody knew what the hell it was," says Bill Hopkins of New York State's substance abuse unit. "Two months later, it was everywhere."

Entering the bloodstream instantly through the entire surface of the lungs, crack produces an immediate euphoria that lasts less than a minute. Addiction is equally rapid, coming after a couple of weeks of use as compared with the eighteen months it takes to turn a regular user of heroin into an addict. Everything was faster with crack—the high, the addiction, and the need for more. The drug spawned violent crime wherever it appeared. But what is most significant about crack is that it was a drug specifically created and targeted for a definite market—the desperate urban poor who could not afford the cocaine snorted by movie stars and celebrity athletes. Hopkins called it a "marketing miracle. Powdered coke for poor black folk. Who couldn't come up with $10?"

It was not only a "marketing miracle" but something of a minor scientific triumph as well. Cocaine decomposes at high temperatures, and it must have taken considerable experimentation to hit on a method that would allow it to burn and produce fumes that could be inhaled. A member of the Cali cartel, Mario Villabona, has testified to meeting the scientist responsible for that triumph—identified only as "Oscar"—who worked for the cartel then led by Gilberto Rodríguez Orejuela, known as the "chess player." Crack was one of his more successful gambits. After saturating the American market, the cartel switched their efforts to Great Britain and continental Europe.

"Designer drugs" and synthetic narcotics may well be the wave of the future. When slight alterations are made to their formulas, designer drugs can enjoy a brief window of "legality" until the law is rewritten to catch up with them. Synthetics are not subject to all the problems associated with cultivation and processing—the vagaries of the weather, transportation of base materials, procurement of precursor chemicals. Control of the production and distribution chain is significantly easier with synthetics, which do not have to travel from the Andes or Myanmar to their final destination. Though they may well be marketed with the same lethal accuracy as crack, the drugs of the early twenty-first century are more likely to be pure laboratory creations like LSD and Ecstasy. And their creators are more likely to be found in Russia and the territories of the former Soviet Union than in South America. In May 1995, *Ogonyok*, the leading Russian newsmagazine, ran a long piece subtitled "Russia Is Becoming the Center for the Production of Synthetic Narcotics" that details the complicity of young chemists in the creation of a variety of synthetics, including the trimethylphentanile known as the "white Chinaman." At one point after the fall of communism, there was considerable alarm about the possibility of suddenly impoverished Russian physicists relocating to foreign countries to assist them with their nuclear weapons programs. The real problem, however, proved to be the chemists who stayed at home and devoted their talents to the creation of new drugs.

Demographics favor the globalized drug trade. American crime rates are now dropping, but criminologists warn this may be largely generational. It is the youngest who are most likely to experiment with drugs and to engage in violent crime. A new surge in that age group is in the offing. By the year 2000 there will be 41 million Americans between the ages of fifteen and twenty-five, and another 4 million by 2010. America has scored considerable successes in the fight against certain drugs—the spread of information, the fear of AIDS, and the aging of the baby boomers have all contributed to the decrease in the number of drug users. However, to a considerable extent, this has been offset by an increase in the number of heavy users. The costs remain staggering. Between 1988 and 1991, 27,112 Americans died from drug overdoses, a few hundred short of the number of American soldiers killed in the Korean War. Intravenous drug use is the leading cause of AIDS, which costs the country more than $10 billion a year. The Colombian cartels and Chinese triads take something like $200 billion a year from the U.S. economy, a sum roughly equal to the U.S. defense budget.

The world's population will jump from 6 billion to 8 billion between 2000 and 2025. More than 95 percent of that increase will come among the poorest of the planet. The richest 20 percent of the world's population already control 83 percent of the wealth, while the poorest 20 percent receive barely 1.4 percent. Thus, the gap between the haves and have-nots is about to make a quantum leap. The drug trade will continue to recruit its agents from among the most enterprising segments of the population and its customers from among the despairing. A vast gulf between the few rich and the many poor cannot be conducive to stability. And so a vicious circle is established—instability favors the narcotics trade, which by flouting laws only further destabilizes a society. Ultimately, this process must result in an authoritarian backlash or the complete corruption of a society.

But aren't there any positive effects of drug money on a nation's economy? Though the drug lords of Colombia did invest vast sums in construction and public works projects, the end results have been less than favorable. In *Global Habit*, Paul Stares writes:

> If previous experience is any guide, the drug industry can impose significant indirect costs on the economies of host nations. In Colombia . . . the influx of foreign currency is believed to have distorted the economy by artificially raising the value of the local currency, which in turn undermined the competitiveness of other export sectors. The recent influx of U.S. currency into Colombia, much of which is believed to be drug related, has caused inflation to rise and rendered subsequent efforts to control it more difficult. With the Colombian peso continuing to appreciate in value relative to the dollar, the demand for imports has also increased, which again has affected domestic producers. Although the flood of dollars has provided Colombia with more capital to repay debts and invest in national infrastructure projects through government-issued securities, much of the local investment of repatriated drug money has apparently not been carried out in productive fashion. Economists argue that local investments have typically been in short-term speculative ventures designed more to launder money than to promote sustained economic growth. The same point has also been made in relation to Chinese and Pakistani drug proceeds.

Like the trances the drugs induce, even their positive effects prove largely illusory, just the sort of twist one should expect from the riches of hell.

6

The Globalization
of Terror

I N THE '60s a wave of fear swept through London when the Bulgarian KGB publicly assassinated a former Bulgarian diplomat with a poison injected by a fine needle concealed at the end of an umbrella. In April 1996 another umbrella seems to have sent similar shock waves through New York City. It is believed that an umbrella belonging to one of the homeless who live in the tunnels of New York City's subway system was left on the tracks and sparked a series of electric outages. There were small explosions, fires, and smoke. In panic, a number of passengers fled the cars for the tunnels, where a misstep leading to contact with the electrified third rail could have cost them their lives. What counts is not the incident itself which, fortunately, resulted in no serious injury or loss of life, but the assumption on the part of many who fled the subway cars that the explosions were caused by terrorist bombs.

The old Chinese saying "Kill one, frighten ten thousand" now applies to these United States. In the last several years America has come to know all the principal strains of terrorism, both foreign (the bombing of the World Trade Center) and domestic (the bombing of the federal building in Oklahoma City), not to mention the work of ideological loners like Ted Kaczynski, the alleged Unabomber.

Americans had become so conditioned to the thought of

terrorism that when TWA Flight 800 exploded in a fireball off Long Island, New York, in July 1996, on the eve of the Centennial Olympic Games in Atlanta, few believed it possible that the loss of 230 lives could be due to metal fatigue or another malfunction. Terrorism just had to be the answer. Then, when a pipe bomb exploded at the open-air festivities at Olympic Park, the answer to the question of who did it remained uncertain, but the specter of terrorism haunted the games for the duration. As a result, even though the cause of the TWA Flight 800 explosion remains as yet uncertain, and no one has been arrested for the Atlanta pipe bomb, the United States has instituted new airport security measures that will affect, and inconvenience, every international passenger for years to come.

A mere ten years ago terrorism seemed a problem endemic to countries with severe internal tensions, like Israel's with the Palestine Liberation Organization or England's with the Irish Republican Army. If Americans were the victims of terrorism, it was more likely to be in the streets of a foreign city or, say, in the skies over Scotland, as was the case when Libyan terrorists blew up Pan Am Flight 103. When I was growing up, terrorism on American soil was unthinkable. The one incident that stands out in my own memory is the attack on Congress in 1954 by Puerto Rican nationalists, and that was an aberration, the exception that only proved the rule that America was immune to the fear and carnage that haunted Europe and the Middle East. All that has changed. Terrorism is now increasingly part of the landscape.

This has occurred despite American law enforcement's very real successes in fighting terror. The fanatics who bombed the World Trade Center were apprehended quickly and prevented from carrying out their plans for further atrocities, such as the bombing of the Holland Tunnel that connects lower Manhattan with New Jersey and is jammed twice a day with commuters. The two racist, anti-government fanatics who allegedly took 168 lives in Oklahoma were arrested within days of the incident. And though it took eighteen years to hunt down the alleged Unabomber, he is finally now behind bars, where he can no longer cripple or kill.

The only problem is that all these terrorists were apprehended after the fact. A good many terrorist plots are nipped in the bud all the time, of course, and, unless exceedingly ambitious in scope, are treated as nonevents by the press. But major successful acts of terrorism, as well as the arrests and trials of terrorists, always top the evening news. Their effect on society is automatically magnified by the media. These acts become ingrained in people's minds, which is why those usually unflappable New Yorkers took to the tracks.

We were not sufficiently prepared for the first real wave of terror that broke out in America and we are not yet prepared for the next. Along with crime, commerce, and communication, terror is going global. The State Department publication *Patterns of Terrorism* notes that although terrorist attacks are now less frequent, they have become more lethal. The Japanese cult Aum Shinrikyo has already broken the psychological barrier against using weapons of mass destruction. The way has been shown. The terrorists of the late '90s and early twenty-first century will use more sophisticated means and thus pose a more virulent threat to the health of democratic societies by increasingly forcing them to trade liberty for security.

Though this country will continue to face danger from religious extremists, homegrown anarchists, and perennial lone-bomber types, they are all in some sense "old news." The terrorists of tomorrow will be better armed and organized. It will take only one mega–terrorist event in any of the great cities of the world to change the world in a single day. As we shall see, that event could be nuclear or could just as easily occur on the Internet, but whether our sense of secure well-being ends with a bang or a whimper will not be the cause of debate.

The Jonathan Institute has studied terrorism for decades. Named for Jonathan Netanyahu, the Israeli commander and brother of Israel's current prime minister who died rescuing Israelis held hostage by terrorists at Entebbe Airport in Uganda, the institute defines terrorism as: "the deliberate and systematic murder, maiming and menacing of the innocent to inspire fear for political ends." This is a good working definition, but terrorism is evolving in these quickly changing times. It is more difficult to define than ever as terrorism blurs with organized criminal activity and becomes less clearly aligned with pariah states such as Iran, North Korea, and Libya, as was true in the 1970s and 1980s.

The blurred distinction between the criminal and the political is evident in any number of revolutionary groups—Peru's Shining Path, which sells coca leaves to purchase plastique explosive; Sri Lanka's Tamil Tigers, who use kidnapping for ransom to finance their fourteen-year "people's war"; the Montana Freemen, who fill their coffers with the proceeds from counterfeit financial instruments and forged checks. Over time, these groups' political agendas merge with their criminal ones, and it becomes difficult to see which agenda is the underlying one. Conversely, many organized criminal groups today employ the methods of traditional terrorism to obtain, protect, and expand their markets. The Sicilian Mafia, with its hit men blowing up crusading judges; the Colombians from Medellín and Cali, with their private paramilitary forces and assassins known as *sicarios;* the Russians, whose contract killers use intelligence tradecraft to carry out bombings and assassinations—all are difficult to distinguish from terrorists in their methods, which are designed, precisely, to terrify as well as to kill.

In our time, terrorism has too often been successful. If one measure is the diffusion of fear, terrorists have done so from the subways of Tokyo to those of Manhattan. And if the criterion is the achievement of stated political ends, terrorists have scored some significant victories there as well, and much sooner than nearly anyone would have predicted.

In his contribution to a symposium-like volume published in 1986 under the title *Terrorism: How the West Can Win,* the noted historian Paul Johnson writes: "What has the PLO, the quintessential terrorist movement of modern times, achieved? After the PLO and the other terrorist movements it succored racked up an appalling total of lives extinguished and property destroyed, how far have they progressed toward achieving their stated political ends? Not at all; in fact they have regressed. The Palestinian state is further away than ever."

Only eleven years have passed since those words appeared in print. If nothing else, this indicates the velocity of change in the late twentieth century. Terrorist organizations with specific political agendas may be encouraged and emboldened by Yasser Arafat's transformation from outlaw to statesman, while those whose only object is to disrupt society require no such "role models." In fact, what most encourages and emboldens terrorists now are the unprecedented opportunities inherent in the new world of porous borders, instant communications, and access to weapons of mass destruction. Like everything else, global terrorism is mutating at a very rapid rate. Failure to prepare for the new strains verges on the suicidal.

Rebels with a Cause

TERRORISM IS SOMETIMES KNOWN as the revenge of the weak, since it is much easier to commit a terrorist act against a foreign enemy than to field an army for a conventional war. My Senate colleague former Foreign Relations Committee chairman Claiborne Pell has been fond of stating that "one man's terrorist is another man's freedom fighter." Senator Pell recognized that one of the greatest dangers of the terrorists is that unlike other criminals, they believe that what they are doing is morally right. They are rebels with a cause.

Those on the lower end of the geopolitical, social, and economic ladders have always had reasons for wanting violent change. What many have lacked was the means to carry out any action to express their rage, and opportune targets. The first great industrial era of the nineteenth century spawned the anarchist movement, the prototype of all modern terrorist groups. The anarchists never commanded much in the way of votes. But they had a substantial impact on the politics of their day, successfully assassinating heads of state and key political figures in Russia, Austria, France, and the United States, provoking a wave of repressive actions, including mass deportations in the United States and summary executions elsewhere. By the late 1920s, the anarchist movement was largely absorbed into the ideological warfare between communism and the West. But the anarchist ideology, the public display of violence for the sake of violence, lives on.

With the end of the superpower struggle, increased attention has fallen on radical Islam. It was twenty-five years ago that the world was treated to the murder of Israeli Olympic athletes in Munich by a group of hooded Palestinian terrorists. Since then, we have witnessed dozens of other horrific incidents, from the murder of a wheelchair-bound Leon Klinghoffer on the Italian cruise ship *Achille Lauro* to the destruction and downing of Pan Am Flight 103 over Lockerbie, Scotland, to the World Trade Center bombing, that have served no purpose but to remind the West of Islamic rage. Angry Islamic extremists are far from the only terrorists: It was dissident Sikhs, for example, who blew up an Air India plane in Canada in the mid-1980s and right-wing homegrown militiamen who allegedly blew up the federal building and children in a day care center in Oklahoma City. The trouble is, with all the explosives available in the world, and the huge number of available targets for anyone willing to kill civilian men, women, and children, any rebel with a cause can decide to be a terrorist. It is not a matter of means, or opportunity—only of desire.

Under U.S. leadership, nations have arrayed themselves to discourage state-sponsored terrorism. We have made such sponsorship a very risky business, as Libya, Iran, and Iraq and their peoples have learned through bitter experience. But as French interior minister Bernard Debré observed in the summer of 1996, today's terrorist networks are far harder to target, owing to their autonomy, lack of clear strategy, and rapid rate of reproduction. Debré concluded that what was necessary to stop them was for states to focus on monitoring banks, computer networks, and weapons trafficking as essential components of detecting terrorist networks as they emerge.

The Big One

CALIFORNIANS REFER to the massive earthquake they fear one day must come as the Big One. And those who monitor global terrorism are now doing much the same, except that what they dread and anticipate could dwarf in damage any spasms of the San Andreas fault. Here the Big One is a nuclear device in the hands of terrorists or a transnational criminal organization.

Various scenarios have been conceived and examined by journalists, which is all to the good—we need to be shocked into awareness of this danger. An article on "loose nukes" published in *Maclean's* in April 1996 opens: "A rusty freighter, controlled by extremists willing to inflict mass slaughter to publicize their cause, steams towards New York City. Hidden beneath tons of scrap metal in its hold, almost undetectable to radioactivity sensors, is a fist-sized ball of plutonium. . . ." *Asiaweek* imagines the jeopardy closer to its part of the world: "In the not-so-distant future, several key officers of the Russian nuclear-powered icebreaker *Northern Star,* based at Murmansk, become infuriated because they haven't been paid for six months. They decide to steal several fuel units containing about 100 kg of highly enriched uranium, and sell them to . . . members of the latest of Japan's 'new religions.' . . ." The result is a nuclear incident in the Ginza District of Tokyo. And projecting future danger onto the past, a *New York Times* Op-Ed piece of April 10, 1996, asks: "What if the bomb that killed 168 people and blasted the Federal building in Oklahoma City . . . had been nuclear?"

These "what-if" scenarios are based on the assumption that Russia's ill-guarded, ill-monitored stockpile of nuclear materials (including everything from weapons to radioactive waste from power plants) will be the source of the new weapon in terrorist hands.

How real is that danger of leakage? In the former Soviet Union, many facilities containing nuclear materials were not kept under especially heavy guard. A chain-link fence and a sign stating that entry was STRICTLY PROHIBITED were more than enough to warn off any Soviet citizen with an ounce of sense. Recent reports indicate that uranium is being stored in the sort of lockers used by students in American high schools. In Murmansk, a Russian naval officer crawled through a hole in the fence surrounding a submarine fuel facility, broke into a locker, and hacked off a ten-pound hunk of enriched uranium, which he hid in his garage. He was caught only when he attempted to find a buyer. Though the scenarios about nuclear terrorism have the aura of slick thrillers about them, the reality will be considerably humbler, more prosaic.

Estimates vary greatly as to how much plutonium and

uranium are scattered around Russia and the territories of the former Soviet Union—in fact, that's part of the problem, no one knows how much is where. Sleek, meticulous efficiency was never one of Russia's outstanding features—before the Soviets, under them, or after. The problem is compounded by vast distances, political disarray, and the lack of funds, political will, and hard information. However, the U.S. government does know that the warheads from the missiles Russia is currently dismantling as part of the START treaties are being added to the estimated 1,500 tons of plutonium and highly enriched uranium stored in hundreds of sites across the country. Only about 20 percent of those have a level of electronic sensors like portal monitors, exit doors with built-in radiation detectors, that would rate as adequate by our standards.

And we also know that in the five years since the red flag came down over the Kremlin, there have been more than eight hundred attempts to smuggle nuclear material out of the Russian and former Soviet republics. In late 1995, twenty-seven crates of Russian beryllium, useful for high-grade nuclear weaponry, were intercepted in Lithuania en route to a buyer in Switzerland who was probably representing North Korea. Guidance gyroscopes from Russian ballistic missiles were seized in a storage shed at Amman airport in Jordan, awaiting transshipment to Iraq. Three former Soviet citizens were arrested in Munich carrying a lead-lined suitcase containing 363 grams of the 4,000 grams of nuclear material needed to make a crude bomb. The material was being offered at $350 million.

Those are just three of the more interesting of the eight hundred examples. Any insurance company actuary examining this situation would no doubt conclude that the Big One was only a matter of time. And that view is supported by studies done for many world leaders. In early February 1994, Germany's federal intelligence agency, the BND, prepared a special eighteen-page report for Chancellor Helmut Kohl on the smuggling and sale of Russian nuclear materials in Germany alone, citing more than two hundred cases. A classified CIA report on "loose nukes" was prepared in 1996 for President Clinton for his April summit with President Yeltsin in Moscow. Testifying to a Senate subcommittee, CIA director John Deutch termed nuclear leakage "a major national security threat."

What is that threat and who might make it? Though some sophisticated training and technology are required to make a nuclear weapon of the primitive Hiroshima type, under the right circumstances fissile material of any sort can kill tens of thousands. "If wrapped around the outside of a conventional explosive device, this material could render an area too contaminated for human life for 8 to 10 years. And intelligence indicates that terrorist groups are studying these ideas," notes Marvin Cetron, the author of *Terrorism 2000: The Future Face of Terrorism*, which was prepared for the Defense Department and predicts the advent of a "superterrorism" marked by the willingness and ability to deploy weapons of mass destruction.

Terrorists are, in my opinion, more likely than transnational criminals to be the ones to shatter the nuclear peace that has lasted from Nagasaki to this day. All the major transnational criminal organizations are thriving precisely because their regular and ordinary businesses are booming. Given the nature of their businesses, they like to keep their heads down, to minimize the risks of attracting any additional attention from governments. They have no pressing reason to engage in the especially provocative activities, like nuclear extortion, that are certain to provoke high-level retaliation. Of course, that does not rule out the possibility that some rogue Russian or Asian outfit might be tempted by the lure of a big score. Russian and other global crime organizations have already proved willing to smuggle and sell nuclear material; there is reason to believe that distribution and sale of such material was one of the main topics at the Italian and Russian mafia summits during 1993 and 1994. It is, however, more likely that a small collection of angry souls with a mission, grievance, and burning faith will be the first to privatize nuclear violence. There are two kinds of groups to fear here: the political and the religious. For the former, terrorism is just politics by other means. For the latter, terrorism becomes the alternative to prayer as a means of demonstrating their faith.

The political use of nuclear material by nonstate groups may already have happened, though not by terrorists per se. In November 1995, Russian government officials and journalists were notified by Chechen rebels that a container of radioactive cesium had been buried in a popular Moscow park. An accompanying videotape instructed them where to dig. And this incident, though more symbolic than actual, also demonstrated that we were wrong to worry only about nuclear material being shipped out of Russia. A terrorist nuclear event could happen even more easily in Moscow than in Tokyo, Bonn, or New York.

We had suspected that former Soviet nuclear material or even weapons were still in the Chechen territory. To some degree, this was even public knowledge. On February 25, 1996, *The New York Times Magazine* ran a cover story about American "global lifesaver and trouble-shooter" Fred Cuny, who disappeared in Chechnya, possibly for having strayed too near a former missile base in Bamut. Before he was killed in April 1996, Chechen leader Dzhokhar Dudayev was interviewed by *Time* magazine:

> TIME: Do you have any weapons of mass destruction?
> DUDAYEV: We won't use them, unless Russia uses nuclear weapons.

That, of course, could be a bluff, but then again so could have been the warning about radioactive cesium in the park.

Fortunately, though they were the first to break the taboo on nuclear terrorism, the Chechens have not yet proved infectious in their example. In fact, the greater danger remains the illicit sale of nuclear materials and expertise to outlaw states like North Korea and, especially, Iraq, which has any number of perceived enemies and real grievances.

Throughout the entire Cold War, we dreaded a nuclear Armageddon that never materialized. The same may well prove the case in this strange new era of post–Cold War terrorism and transnational crime. The reasons are utterly practical. Those wishing to create havoc, whether for purposes of profit or politics, have simpler, cheaper, and more easily available means at their disposal. Nukes are expensive and high-risk, and, when compared with certain chemical and biological weapons, can seem as crude and quaintly dated as Nikita Khrushchev banging his shoe at the United Nations.

Chemical Kamikazes and Communications Commandos

IT IS A TRUISM that religious cults have always been with us. It is also, unfortunately, a recurrent problem with messianic cults that from time to time they predict a violent confrontation with the world. Some of these cults, like the Branch Davidians of Waco, Texas, headed by David Koresh in 1993, and the Jonestown families in Guyana in 1978, even bring about their own apocalypse. But new in our globalized world is the ability of such cults to project their visions of Armageddon on a canvas that in reality can extend to entire societies.

March 20, 1995, is a date of seminal importance in the history of terrorism. The religious cult Aum Shinrikyo's sarin nerve-gas attack on the Tokyo subway, which killed 12 and injured 3,796, not only shattered Japan's myth of living in a secure society, it also breached the boundary on the use of chemical weapons of mass destruction by terrorists. The attack could well have been nuclear. "If you have a sect that is reasonably rich and wants to cause mischief, they just might be able to use a nuclear weapon," says Fred Iklé of the Center for Strategic and International Studies in Washington. There are indications that Aum was looking in that direction as well. Documents confiscated from the cult's "defense minister," Kibe Tetsuya, include notations on the cost of "nuclear heads"—$200,000 for secondhand, $1 million for a new one. Police also seized documents concerning uranium enrichment technology when raiding the sect's headquarters near Mount Fuji. Aum's propaganda also included frequent references to a nuclear holocaust that the leader, Shoko Asahara, predicted would occur between 1999 and 2003. Given the money, laboratories, and scientific expertise at his disposal, he could well have made this a self-fulfilling prophecy. The current trial of the cult may reveal whether it possessed any serious intentions along the nuclear line, but it already is known that the sect had strong connections with Russia, where the sect did extensive business, claimed 30,000 members, and owned a Russian-manufactured helicopter. Documents found at Aum's

Japanese headquarters showed that the cult was negotiating purchases of military equipment and weapons, transactions interrupted only by the Japanese raids and the arrests of Aum's officers.

Whatever their long-range intentions may have been, when the cult decided to launch its attack on Japanese society, it chose the deadly nerve gas sarin, the ingredients for which were legally available in Japan, just as the materials that went into the bomb that destroyed the federal building in Oklahoma City could be purchased without great difficulty in the United States. Robert Gates, former director of the CIA, has defined the problem: "When you talk about chemical and biological weapons in particular, a lot of them can be made in your basement, so the idea of keeping them out of terrorist hands altogether is simply not technologically feasible." For example, police in Columbus, Ohio, recently investigated a suspected member of the white supremacist group Aryan Nation who worked as a lab technician and used his company's certification by the Food and Drug Administration to obtain otherwise banned biological materials to purchase three vials of bubonic plague bacteria. U.S. law-enforcement, military, and intelligence agencies treat the biological threat quite seriously. The FBI and the Energy Department have already conducted mock exercises premised on the release of a biological agent in the New York City subways.

It is not only the availability of materials that can be transformed into explosives or poisons that presents the problem here; it is also the availability of the information to do so that counts. The opening of borders to international commerce and the information highway have benefited terrorists every bit as much as they have helped legitimate businesspeople and criminals. You don't have to surf the Net very long to be able to find such information. Two Massachusetts teenagers learned this lesson the hard way on August 7, 1996, when they suffered disfiguring burns in an explosion they produced from basic household ingredients after following a recipe they picked up at home on-line for making a bomb.

Free trade and the free flow of information are inextricably linked. I vigorously support international trade, having voted to expand free trade with Mexico and Canada through the North American Free Trade Agreement (NAFTA), and to strengthen the World Trade Organization through the recent global General Agreement on Tariffs and Trade (GATT). But unlike many free-trade supporters, I see that there are costs as well as benefits to global trade, and one of the biggest is that it literally brings crime and terrorism right to our doorstep.

The Colombian cocaine kingpins know this. That is why they bought up businesses in northern Mexico in 1992 and 1993 as it became clear that legitimate cross-border trade would expand enormously following the creation of a North American free trade area. They knew that once they were in Mexico, they would be able to move goods—legally and illegally—into the United States with little interference by U.S. customs inspectors. The barriers imposed by customs at a time when tariffs still required careful inspections were far from perfect. Eliminating any tax and trade reasons for inspection, as NAFTA did, made detection of smuggled goods among the flood of legitimate goods even harder.

The Japanese *yakuza* know about the criminal harvest free trade reaps. They sell pirated Western software throughout the Asian Pacific rim, thus financing their other illegal ventures.

Free trade goes well beyond the movement of goods; ideas and information also flow back and forth. This intellectual commerce contributed to the demise of the Soviet Union and the transformation of Latin America from nations beset by revolutions, military dictatorships, and guerrilla wars to representative democracies where, for the most part, the center seems to be holding. But it also opens the way to new dangers. There were good reasons for the United States to fight to keep new technologies away from the old Soviet Union and its allies. Technologies can be abused, and not everyone can be trusted. Yet in an era of free trade, it is impossible to keep anything away from whoever is truly determined to obtain it. In 1995 and 1996 we have seen German hackers selling classified U.S. intelligence to the successors of the KGB, and criminals in Argentina accessing the financial records of kidnapping victims electronically. The same computer networks that once provided information to dissident groups are now used to penetrate classified government databases. Bookstores sell how-to books on techniques for industrial espionage, telephone tapping, and even bombmaking. Purchasers range from high-school computer nerds to considerably more dangerous characters. Take the motley assortment of nobodies who on February 26, 1993, bombed the World Trade Center. These nobodies were people who came to the United States from halfway around the world. Yet even as they retained their political views, religious ideas, and ties to their home countries, they also had access to the full array of information freely available to anyone in the United States with decent library skills. Ordinarily, this access to information is a marvelous aspect of modern life. But as with the free trade in goods, there is a dark side to the free trade of information. In this case, a small group of adherents to a blind Muslim cleric, operating without the support of any government, was able to shut down Wall Street and strike terror into the heart of America's financial district.

International trade and communication are the most powerful sources of social, cultural, and economic change in the world today. Economic globalization is revolutionizing the distribution of jobs and pay scales, raising standards of living, liberating women, bringing down and raising governments, and introducing marvelous but disturbing new choices—of goods, services, lifestyles, and beliefs—into still traditional cultures like those of Egyptian Muslims.

Change so sudden, so deep, so all-encompassing is bound to strain societies to the breaking point—and beyond. While many people embrace such change, equal numbers fear it. They clutch fanatically, desperately, at the nearest available metaphysical and moral certainties—most often religious fundamentalism or fanatic nationalism—hoping to turn back the future. The most extreme among them use crime as a tactic—not crime as we ordinarily think of it, lawbreaking for profit, but crime for vengeance, as retribution or holy war. And their favorite instrument is terrorism.

But, as the case of the alleged Unabomber amply demonstrates, it is not only Third World societies undergoing a rapid and confusing transition to modernity that produce this phenomenon. Though he was an extreme case of the loner, Ted Kaczynski nevertheless expressed in his manifesto sentiments that find increasing resonance among the disenfranchised or disaffected segments of the American population: "The Industrial Revolution and its consequences have been a disaster for the human race. They have greatly increased the life-expectancy of those of us who live in 'advanced' countries, but they have destabilized society, have subjected human beings to indignities, have led to widespread psychological suffering (in the Third World to physical suffering as well) and have inflicted severe damage on the natural world."

Indeed, there is a general sense of displeasure with technology that accompanies its obvious benefits. It is shared by everyone who has lost a job to a computer and everyone who, saying, "I finally got a human on the line," is rebelling against that sense of cool impersonality that technology has infused into social and commercial relations. But this is nothing new. It has been with us since 1811, when the Luddites, English textile weavers displaced by the invention of the automatic shuttle loom, smashed those machines in an inchoate revolt against the Industrial Revolution. And the fears of science's fateful and forbidden tinkering with nature have been reflected by high culture in works like Henry David Thoreau's *Walden* and in popular culture by everything from Mary Shelley's novel *Frankenstein*, published more than 150 years ago, to HAL, the robot gone wild in Stanley Kubrick's classic film *2001*.

Those who revolt against the effects of science and technology on human life need not be displaced workers or religious fanatics. Ted Kaczynski held a Ph.D. in mathematics and Aum Shinrikyo numbered several well-educated scientists among its members, a fact that Japanese society found particularly disturbing. As we have seen, scientists are not morally immune to the blandishments of crime—the cocaine labs of Colombia and the synthetic drug factories in Russia depend on educated people —and, for all their rationality, scientists are still subject to the passions of faith, the temptations of greed, and the dark allure of vengeance.

In fact, a danger greater than nuclear, biological, or chemical terrorism may be posed by those with no more than a powerful computer, a keen mind, and an undying grudge. The pen may not have been mightier than the sword, but the keyboard could well prove to be. Technology-driven societies are vulnerable in their sophistication. The basic utilities of every city—electricity, gas, water—are to a considerable extent dependent on their own computer systems. No matter how complex the encryption, the unbreakable code has yet to be devised. "There is no such thing as a secure network, except possibly for a Department of Defense operation," says James Kates, a Florida security consultant with

Janus Associates, which hacks clients' systems to uncover security flaws. The word "possibly" was well chosen: During Desert Storm, Dutch hackers penetrated the Pentagon's computers and were able to track plans for troop movements. Twenty-five percent of the Pentagon's logistics communications are uncoded and sent on the Internet. Those Dutch hackers had offered their services to Saddam Hussein, who wasn't interested—that time around.

Information warfare has become a hot issue. The CIA and the Pentagon have groups devoted to information warfare— how governments can use it to achieve military or economic victories and what the United States can do to defend against it. The DISA, the Defense Information Systems Agency, recently reported results of "test" penetrations of over eight thousand Department of Defense computers using readily available hacker tools. The results were hardly encouraging. Eighty-eight percent of all attempts were successful and only 5 percent of those were detected. And even when the results of those penetrations are discovered it is exceedingly difficult to determine whether penetration was a mistake, a hardware or software problem, a criminal act, or an attack by an enemy state.

As the world's reliance on its technological infrastructure grows greater with each nanosecond, the problems become increasingly obvious: Criminals are attracted to going on-line because, increasingly, on-line is where the big money is. Every bank and major financial institution is on-line twenty-four hours a day, just as are the CIA, the Federal Reserve, credit and cash services, and telecommunications companies. The rapid and haphazard growth of this electronic infrastructure means that, in the words of a government report, it is "unevenly protected against intrusion and malevolent activity (in fact, there has been considerable resistance to governmental protections)," and the ability to access the Net remotely makes it nearly impossible to identify and locate illicit users. For example, the European Union Bank of Antigua, the West Indies—which has nothing to do with Europe, let alone the real European Union—was created with a $1 million investment from a Russian bank that the CIA has linked to organized crime. It consists mainly of a rather elegant Web site on the Internet that offers banking services by computer. Anyone with a personal computer, anywhere in the world, may use a European Union Bank account to create new, untraceable corporations with phony officers and directors; obtain credit cards whose billings exist solely in cyberspace; and, in general, engage in a variety of secret transactions, including fraud and money laundering, limited only by the user's imagination and tax evasion requirements.

Already, the European Union Bank is said to be under investigation by the FBI and Internal Revenue Service, as well as a variety of intelligence agencies. But the investigators have their work cut out for them. The bank's corporate records in Antigua show little, and its computer server isn't even located there, but in a country in a different part of the world entirely. Where do you send the bank examiners? Even if those bank examiners were themselves cybernetic, chances are they would remain a technological step or two behind the criminals. After all, the private sector pays a lot better than the public sector, and it has been decades since "the best and the brightest" chose to devote their services to the public interest rather than to those willing to pay the highest-going market rates.

Reduced government spending on technology in the wake of congressional funding cuts has made the problem worse. For instance, the U.S. Department of State still relies on state-of-the-art 1978 Wang computers for its global communications. These computers were retired in the private sector more than a decade ago, are at least three generations out of date, cannot gain access to the Internet, and increasingly have to be cannibalized when their parts break down, since replacement parts are no longer being manufactured. With the Congress unwilling to fund new computers, U.S. diplomats cannot communicate with the FBI or the CIA by e-mail, and have to rely on the decades-old technique of reporting by cable, just as they did in the era of the telegraph. As the U.S. government concluded in its 1996 report on the topic, "acquisition cycles of new equipment with law enforcement, and the government in general, have seriously lagged the ability of criminals to adopt and adapt new techniques and equipment."

André Bacard, author of *The Computer Privacy Handbook*, prophesied in a February 1996 interview: "When the common criminal becomes computer-literate, America will be in trouble." But criminals have already discovered the pleasures and profit of theft by computer. Fast, clean, and relatively safe, it is one of the fastest-growing areas of crime—if not *the* fastest-growing—

in most technologically sophisticated societies. The problem here is that hard, reliable statistics are difficult to come by—some companies are embarrassed by their violability and prefer to keep their losses to themselves. In 1995 theft by computer was known to be the fastest-growing area of criminal activity in Britain, where losses were estimated at some 1 billion pounds ($1.5 billion U.S.).

On June 5, 1996, *The Times* of London revealed that City of London financial institutions had paid huge sums to international gangs, which the newspaper called "cyber-terrorists." *The Times* charged that during the previous three years, British brokerage firms, blue-chip banks, and defense firms had paid tens of millions of pounds at a time in extortion money to criminals who had penetrated their computers and threatened to wreak havoc with their records. In each incident, the gangs demonstrated they had the capacity to crash the target's computers, forcing the victim to transfer money to offshore bank accounts, where the gang members immediately transferred it into financial cyberspace and untraceable oblivion.

Here at home, Citibank, which transfers electronically around $500 billion a day, was penetrated in 1995 by Russian criminal hackers who had illegally transferred $12 million to accounts in the United States, Finland, Germany, Israel, the Netherlands, Russia, and Switzerland, and withdrew $400,000 before they were apprehended. In 1995 the U.S. Computer Emergency Response Team noted a twentyfold increase in the number of people hacking their way into private networks—more than 2,300 incidents.

John Lee, a founder of the Masters of Deception hacker group, said he could change credit-card records as well as utility and rent rates; charge plane tickets, hotels, and meals; and obtain insider trading information by violating and manipulating electronic communications systems. Lee, who never admitted any wrongdoing yet spent a year in jail, boasted that he could commit a crime "with five keystrokes" of his computer.

The creation of encrypted systems for business has already become a multimillion-dollar worldwide industry. In its 1995 *Internet Security Survey*, the Computer Security Institute of San Francisco estimated that one out of every five Net sites had suffered a security breach in the relatively brief period of the Net's existence, and for that reason it predicted that sales of anti-hacker software will soar from $1.1 billion in 1995 to $16.2 billion by 2000. Motorola alone is spending millions to secure everything from its e-mail to chip designs and business strategy. One executive involved in the creation of the system says, "We constantly have attempts to break into our computers from people who are politically or financially motivated, as well as the merely curious."

The big players are already catching on. IBM, whose Swift transfer system handles $3 trillion a day, protects its system with encryption devices supplied by Cylink, the first major company to provide the commercial sector with end-to-end communication and encryption security. Founded in 1984 (of all years), Cylink provides banks, businesses, and utilities with encryption devices and systems that afford them protection against criminals, terrorists, and the sort of computer anarchist whose motive is not profit or politics but a simple urge to disrupt and destroy. The real source of the security vulnerability is that many businesses prefer to use the Internet for a portion of their operations because of the considerably cheaper costs involved. For example, a leased line costs $1,000 a month, whereas on the Net this service runs only some $20. But, as Dr. Howard Morgan, a director and member of Cylink's board, has piquantly remarked: "Unprotected communications over the Internet are more dangerous than unsafe sex."

And wherever the criminals are, the terrorists cannot be far behind. An *Awareness Document* published by the Department of Defense as far back as September 1993 observes that hackers —whether a nerd who engages in mischievous anarchy or the outright criminal type—could, if employed by terrorists, cripple the country's telephone system and "create significant public health and safety problems, and cause serious economic shocks."

Information warfare, cyberterrorism, has, like the six-gun, been called the "great equalizer." Former Pentagon communications chief Donald Latham observes that a "few very smart guys with computer workstations and modems could endanger lives and cause great economic disruption."

What would be the principal attack routes?

Information Warfare for Dummies: A Guide for the Perplexed, a report prepared by Department of Defense contractor TRW in Texas and accessible over the Net during the summer of 1996, notes four basic types of network penetration:

- insertion of malicious code (viruses, worms, etc.)
- theft of information
- manipulation of information
- denial of service

A virus could infect any system with chaos and bring it to its knees—Wall Street, the phone system, air traffic control. Information theft can clearly cause serious injury to an enemy, as Saddam Hussein would have discovered had he taken the Dutch hackers up on their offer. Disinformation, the insertion of incorrect or misleading information into a system, can be as dangerous and difficult to detect as malicious software code. Denial of service has already been practiced as an instrument of protest or terrorist weapon; the definition, as always, depends on your politics. What isn't subject to argument is how effective denial of service can be. That was demonstrated in December 1995 when, outraged by French nuclear testing, Italian protesters launched a worldwide campaign to swamp the French government's World Wide Web servers and forced them to shut down. A similar event occurred in Mexico in connection with the guerrilla (Zapatista) leader Subcomandante Marcos, who always carries a laptop, which he plugs into the cigarette lighter of an old pickup truck. According to a *Washington Post* article, "When federal police raided alleged Zapatista safe houses in Mexico City and the southern states of Veracruz . . . they found as many computer diskettes as bullets." When President Ernesto Zedillo announced a military offensive to capture the ski-masked Zapatista leader, "cyberpeaceniks" appealed on the Net for faxes to be sent to the president imploring him to call off the campaign. Within hours, Zedillo's fax machine either broke down or was turned off, as the appeals came streaming in. He also called back his troops.

In a small way, the Central Intelligence Agency has already been hit by computer attack. Its Web site had to be shut down in September 1996 when hackers wishing to make a political statement flooded the site with electronic contacts as a means of overloading it. The CIA, with all of its technical expertise, was unable to save the site and reopen it. Instead, the agency was forced to move the site to a different location on the Web entirely, starting anew.

Former CIA deputy director William Studeman has stated that "massive networking makes the U.S. the world's most vulnerable target for information warfare," pointing out that our systems could be attacked by drug traffickers, organized crime, computer vandals, disgruntled employees, or paid professionals. And they need not necessarily use computers to damage our communications technology. The Army's Force XXI document that envisions land warfare in the twenty-first century—and is itself available on the Internet—notes a new weapon, nonnuclear electromagnetic pulse generators (EMPs). *Information Warfare for Dummies* explains:

> The high-energy pulse emitted by an EMP bomb can temporarily or permanently disable all electronic systems, including computers, for a radius of several kilometers. Put simply, EMP weaponry *fries* electronic circuitry. EMP weapons can be launched by airborne platforms, or detonated inside information centers (banks, corporate headquarters, telephone exchanges, military command posts). The explosion needed to trigger the electromagnetic pulse apparently is minor compared to a conventional blast, theoretically resulting in fewer human casualties.

If it takes a stretch to imagine the threats posed to our national security by transnational crime, little effort is needed to realize that terrorism goes right for the jugular. If the charges against Ted Kaczynski are accurate, it may have been only his distaste for modern technology that prevented him from attaining the status of first major cyberterrorist, but the odds are that someone else will yet claim that "honor."

Liberty versus Security

THE OPEN ARCHITECTURE of a wired world, where anyone can link up with anyone, anywhere, on the Internet, would seem to be the embodiment of the kind of open society that the United States has always championed as the model for democracy. Indeed, what could be more democratic than a system in which we can publish any information we want, and anyone who wants to read it can check the information out?

Electronic communication systems and democracies are a natural match. Functioning on the same principles, they reinforce each other's strengths. More than thirty years ago the passage of the Freedom of Information Act (FOIA) in the United States took the principle of government disclosure and created the presumption that most government documents are releasable to the public. But FOIA was always too labor intensive, and too slow, to make it very useful until the Internet came along. The Net is only a few years old. Yet already, literally millions of U.S. government documents have been put on-line, from most IRS tax forms to the daily press briefings at the State Department. So far, so good. But the freedom of the Net also creates real risks. In October 1996 the Federation of American Scientists, a Washington public-interest lobbying group, put a number of authentic "top-secret" documents on its Web site. The documents, relating to U.S. ballistic missile defense systems, had been obtained by a journalist from a disgruntled federal employee. A threat to the national security? Maybe, maybe not. But the precedent has been set, and once information enters the Net, this is a genie that cannot be rebottled.

That is why governments, banks, businesses, criminals, and terrorists alike all need to ensure that the information they transmit over the wires is adequately protected. On the one hand, they each want their information to be encrypted so no one can read (or manipulate) it without permission. On the other hand, there is the desire to prevent counterfeiting of real information —from the counterfeiting of compact discs and computer software to the counterfeiting of money itself electronically through financial data manipulation.

Thus, protecting your data becomes essential: Computer security becomes ever more important as computer technology becomes ever more ubiquitous. Any surge in computer theft or computer terrorism threatens everyone's security, not just that of Citibank or the CIA. What happens if a hacker assault wipes out everyone's access to ATMs in a single afternoon? Or if a terrorist attack on U.S. government computers creates readings suggesting, falsely, that a real terrorist attack has begun, requiring an immediate military response. So far, we have been lucky. No worst-case scenario has yet come close to being reality. Our computer age has seen financial meltdowns of only a few billion dollars at a time through the market manipulations of dishonest traders, not terrorists. But what if the terrorists do target our information systems?

Government security experts from the G-7 major industrial countries continue to meet, working to come up with responses. The kind of measures they are talking about indeed threaten to trade our freedom and privacy for personal and social safety. The picture ID we now must show in order to board a plane might become a necessity in any number of daily situations, instead of just the irritating exception it currently is. Cards verifying your identity may well prove necessary for gaining access to the computer system where you work. Security experts call this biometrics. Biometrics take a fingerprint or the pattern of a human retina and place the original on an ID or credit card. The original must match the user of the card in order for it to be honored. This is potentially a great way to reduce credit card fraud. But it also creates a real risk of abuse: Do we want businesses and governments to be able to monitor our every movement with personal biometric data?

Already, according to a 1996 survey, 80 percent of Americans feel that they have "lost all control" over personal information about themselves. In truth, databases containing information on us as consumers are routinely bought and sold, our movements are monitored by video cameras in malls, and our communications, both voice and electronic, are subject to monitoring at work.

The government's response to the terrorist problem threatens to take the concern about loss of privacy to another level. The Clinton administration has considered two different approaches to the problem of data security and the government's need to know. The first approach, known as the clipper chip, was proposed by the administration in April 1993 and provoked a firestorm of controversy. The chip would have made it possible for the government, upon receiving permission from a court, to decrypt all communications of a target by giving the government the equivalent of a skeleton key to all encrypted data. When protests ensured the death of that idea, the administration suggested instead that the skeleton key be held by a nongovernment person in what was called the key-escrow system. The idea was that the third person would provide only the key upon receipt of an appropriate court order. Civil libertarian groups shot this idea down, too, arguing that it would create an electronic Big Brother as surely as would the clipper chip. As *Wired*, a magazine for aficionados of technology, has declared, "Trusting the government with your privacy is like having a Peeping Tom install your window blinds." But one would be hard-pressed to find a single grieving relative of those killed in the bombings of the World Trade Center in New York or the federal building in Oklahoma City who would not have gladly sacrificed a measure of personal privacy if it could have saved a loved one.

So far, governments have reached no consensus on how to keep track of criminals electronically. In the meantime, France has already made it illegal for the private sector to use strong cryptography techniques. The United Kingdom classifies sophisticated security programs as munitions, as does the United States, and subjects them to rigid export restrictions even with the European Union. In the end, as Nanette Di Tosto of Bankers Trust Company says, "There has to be a global policy on cryptography. . . ."

Personally, I doubt that any technology fix will ensure that governments have access to encrypted information. Neither a clipper chip nor key-escrow system, even if universally accepted, is going to stop some technowhiz from marketing a system to get around the system. What governments need to do is devote enough resources to keep up with high-tech advances, to ensure that they keep up with the private sector. Historically, the United States has done this with military and intelligence spending, which, driven by the Cold War, provided us with a real technological edge. Indeed, the Net itself owes its existence to U.S. defense spending. It was the Pentagon, through the Defense Advanced Research Projects Agency (DARPA), that created ARPANET, the ancestor of today's World Wide Web. Rather than trying to confine technology, an approach destined for failure, the United States needs to stay on the cutting edge of technology itself. Governments that fail to do so by hiring the best and brightest computer software, hardware, and cryptological specialists will be guaranteeing their own obsolescence.

7

Human Contraband

A MAN'S HOME is hardly his castle if strangers are climbing over the front fence, camping out in the backyard, or walking off with the family silver. By the same token, a country's ability to control its borders is one measure of the health and vigor of its sovereignty. But it is even more than a measure. As President Clinton observed in a memorandum for the heads of executive departments and agencies on the subject of deterring illegal immigration: "It is a fundamental right and duty for a nation to protect the integrity of its borders and its laws. This Administration shall stand firm against illegal immigration and the continued abuse of our immigration laws. By closing the back door to illegal immigration, we will continue to open the front door to legal immigrants."

But immigration is a complex and sensitive issue. Complex if only because nearly half of this country's illegal immigrants entered the United States legally and stayed on after their visas expired. Sensitive because America has always been of two minds about immigration. Our noblest sentiments on the subject were voiced by Emma Lazarus, herself the daughter of Jewish immigrants, and are inscribed in bronze on the pedestal of the Statue of Liberty:

> *Give me your tired, your poor,*
> *Your huddled masses, yearning to breathe free,*

The wretched refuse of your teeming shore.
Send these, the homeless, tempest-tost to me,
I lift my lamp beside the golden door!

But in the years since those lines were written, the world has become increasingly tempestuous and we have plenty of homeless of our own. While welcoming immigrants, some Americans have also displayed a convenient amnesia about their own origins mixed with jingoism and economic fear. That attitude is hardly new. In the words of a popular nineteenth-century ditty:

O workingmen dear, and did you hear
The news that's goin' round?
Another China steamer
Has landed here in town . . .
O, California's coming down,
As you can plainly see.
They are hiring all the Chinamen
and discharging you and me. . . .

But those Chinese were legal immigrants. The problem today, as we shall examine in some detail, is the large number of mainland Chinese who, fleeing oppression or seeking opportunity, are arriving in this country packed in the holds of steamers or in the trunks of cars or, supplied with forged documents, on regularly scheduled flights to American airports. The problem is not limited to illegal Chinese aliens, of course. It was not long ago that the bodies of Haitians who failed to make the perilous crossing from their island to this country were washing up on Florida's beaches. And footage of Mexicans penetrating America's southern border almost at will has long been a staple of the evening news.

Though the issues and ramifications of illegal immigration are complex, the origins of the problem are relatively simple. As we have already noted, the current and coming surge in the world's population is almost entirely among the planet's poor. "How many poor I see!" said the English theologian and hymn writer Isaac Watts (1674–1748), but today's poor are different

THE NEW WAR   135

from those of ages past. Modern communications provide them with information about places where life is supposedly better, and the availability of cheap transportation allows them to get there. The same permeable borders that permit the free flow of goods and ideas also allow for the smuggling of human beings. The social and political upheaval of our times and the transformation of communities into new economic patterns due to globalization of both production and markets have created large segments of the dispossessed, the desperate, the driven. None of this is any secret, least of all to the transnational criminal organizations that are always quick to detect new sources of potential profit. Given the demographics, human contraband is a growth industry.

How It Works

"THIS IS THE BUSINESS we chose," says the Meyer Lansky character in *The Godfather*. What exactly is the business the people smugglers have chosen?

The trade in human contraband has been described as "low risk, high gain," which is always an attractive proposition. It is low risk for two main reasons. First, though the United States, in the words of President Clinton, makes "strategic use of sensors, night scopes, helicopters, light planes, all-terrain vehicles, fingerprinting, and automated record keeping," the fact remains that we have total borders that measure some 8,100 miles, one third of the way around the world at the equator. Five hundred million people enter this country every year. The major airports handle more than a thousand landings a day. And the five thousand trucks entering from Mexico each day, of which, as stated earlier, only two hundred are inspected, could just as easily be hauling a shipment of humans as bales of marijuana or bricks of cocaine.

Second, in the United States and Western Europe, penalties for smuggling people are relatively lenient in comparison with those for the smuggling or distribution of narcotics—a few years for the alien smugglers, compared to life for the narcotics kingpins. In most of the rest of the world, there is no penalty at all. The trade is legal, so the smugglers can plan and carry out their trade from sanctuaries in complete safety, without risk or consequences. The people who entice and smuggle the human contraband are necessarily point men. With few exceptions, the big bosses do not jeopardize themselves by engaging in direct action. Those point men, usually from the depths of society, do not find a stretch in an American prison particularly daunting. Medical care, television, and exercise facilities are provided, and, in some prisons, drugs are readily available. "Three hots and a cot" is how some prisoners refer to the provision of meals and bedding.

The smuggling of human beings is not only low risk, it's high gain. Worldwide profits to smugglers now run in the neighborhood of $7 billion a year. As a rule, it costs a Chinese national in the neighborhood of $30,000 to be smuggled into the United States. Only 100,000 Chinese are smuggled into the country per year, compared with the much greater figures for Latin Americans crossing illegally through Mexico. (In fiscal 1994, almost 1 million illegal aliens were apprehended at the Mexican and Canadian borders, nearly 99 percent of whom were Mexicans.) Yet, those 100,000 Chinese paying $30,000 apiece amounts to a tidy $3 billion a year. And that makes "high gain" no misnomer.

Of course, very few of those Chinese have the $30,000 to pay. No problem, say the smugglers (known as snakeheads). They can easily earn the money in America, where, as everybody knows, hard work quickly produces great wealth. The reality is that these people become indentured servants to criminal organizations, or to those willing to rent people from such organizations. Many eke out a living in sweatshops, never reducing the debt by any significant amount. The more attractive women among them choose—or, more often, are forced into—prostitution. Others elect a life of crime as the fastest way of buying back their freedom. Some of them engage in the theft of high-end consumer products, which are then shipped back to China for sale. Those goods are also used to dazzle others with the opulence of America and make them eager to assume the $30,000 debt.

Most of the Chinese smuggled into this country are from the maritime province of Fujian. Historically, that location meant that the Fujianese (also known as Fukienese) were always the most seagoing of the Chinese and, as we have seen, are the most prominent group in the worldwide Chinese diaspora.

But the conditions under which they travel make the steerage used by thousands of previous immigrants seem positively luxurious. It would take a Joseph Conrad to describe the squalor and brutality aboard those ships. America did catch one vivid glimpse of the world of human contraband on June 6, 1993, when a rusty freighter, the *Golden Venture*, whose hold contained some three hundred desperate Chinese, ran aground off the Rockaway peninsula of Queens, New York. The sight of young men clad only in underwear leaping to their death in the chilly waters became one of those images that are seared into the mind, signatures of events.

But in the end it's the statistics that tell the real story. William Kleinknecht puts it like this in *The New Ethnic Mobs*:

At the time the *Golden Venture* ran aground, U.S. immigration officials had intelligence that 24 more ships were on their way to the United States, each packed with illegal Fujianese. In the previous 22 months, authorities had intercepted 14 such ships around the country, and no one could even estimate how many might have gotten through undetected. Four days before the *Golden Venture* arrived, the Coast Guard seized two fishing trawlers with 200 illegals aboard as they landed 60 miles apart on the northern coast of California. The previous month, a freighter dropped 200 illegal immigrants at the foot of San Francisco's Golden Gate Bridge. Of these, 125 were seized by authorities, but 75 escaped into the darkness.

One of the first major smugglers was a woman, Cheng Chui Ping, who had amassed a fortune of $30 million by the time she was arrested by U.S. federal authorities at the Canadian border in 1990. After four months in jail, she was back in business in a building on East Broadway in Manhattan for which she had paid $3 million in cash. Known as Big Sister Ping, she is a hero back home for helping people find a "better life." She compensates the victim's family if anyone dies on the trip, and those who are apprehended and deported go right to the top of the list of those next to be smuggled into America. So what could there be to complain about—besides the deception, the life of debt and misery, not to mention those who happened to die en route? But, in fact, complaints are few—the illegals have little reason to trust the American police because of a general fear of the authorities and a specific fear of deportation.

Some steps have been taken to dispel that fear. On August 7, 1994, President Clinton announced a new policy permitting nationals of the People's Republic of China who enter the United States illegally to remain here even if their claims for political asylum are denied. PRC nationals will not be deported from the United States if they can prove they have suffered, or might suffer, severe harm as a result of the PRC government's one-child policy.

However, if they inform on the criminals who trafficked them, illegal immigrants must still fear reprisals against their relatives back home. So President Clinton's policy may have the unwanted effect of emboldening smugglers. As an executive intelligence brief, *Potential Areas of Concern for the U.S. Immigration and Naturalization Service*, notes: "PRC alien smugglers worldwide are aware of President Clinton's policy change. Once the aliens arrive, they will be able to remain."

In the final days of the 104th Congress in September 1996, Republicans, determined to punish legal immigrants by denying their children access to public schools, continued to fight for protections for illegal immigrants fleeing China on the ground that they wanted to have more children. The final legislative compromise, which satisfied no one, gives immigration officials new powers to get rid of illegals, but also allows illegals to delay deportations through spurious asylum claims. Meanwhile, as these words are written, our coast guard has spotted another ship from South China, with a crew from Taiwan and hundreds of illegals, sailing toward our shores and approaching Bermuda. At a cost of millions of dollars, they will intercept the boat and send the passengers back to Wake Island or Guam or another U.S. facility. There the illegals will stay, as guests of the U.S.

taxpayers, until we can convince the government of China to take their people back, and the government of Taiwan to crack down on the traffickers.

But it is not only the foolish and the desperate who fill the holds of the squalid steamers ferrying human contraband. Each shipment also includes low-level gangsters who enforce obedience en route and later either brutalize the illegals to keep them paying or murder them if they do not. Other gangsters are also dispatched here to swell the ranks of the major criminal organizations engaged in smuggling among other criminal enterprises, like the blandly named Fukienese Residents' Association or the more aptly named Fuk Ching gang.

All of China's current crises—in population, politics, and economic life, where the benefits are great but too few to go around—will continue to feed the trade in human contraband. But China is hardly the sole source of the problem.

Other Players

RUSSIA

Sheremetyevo 2, Moscow's international airport, often looks more like a refugee camp than a jet terminal. Whole families camp out for days on blankets, eating and sleeping there while awaiting permission to stay in Russia or move on to Europe or the United States. At present, it is estimated that some 60,000 Chinese nationals are illegally residing in Moscow, many of whom wish to travel to the United States. The cheapest and most popular routes from China all pass through Moscow.

The overall number of aliens in Russia from countries outside the territories of the former USSR is somewhere between 300,000 and 500,000, most of whom reside in and around Moscow and St. Petersburg. Most of these "transit migrants" entered Russia legally. They fall into three categories: First are students—mainly Afghans, Cubans, Ethiopians, Iraqis, and Somalis—who matriculated at Russian institutions of higher learning and are reluctant to return to their countries of origin. The second group is made up of foreign workers—chiefly from China, Korea, and Vietnam—who did not return home when their contracts expired. The third consists of asylum seekers, numbering around 40,000 from some thirty-eight countries, including Afghanistan, Sri Lanka, Iraq, Angola, Somalia, and Ethiopia. Russian customs and border guard officials, once considered among the most formidable in the world, are now simply overwhelmed by the flood of traffic and the lack of manpower.

The Russian Mafiyas have discovered a new business delivered to their doorstep by the liberal visa laws—and easily corruptible officials—of the new Russia. Those Mafiyas have now begun cooperating with the Chinese triads in the smuggling of human contraband, another instance of the natural alliances formed between such transnational criminal organizations. They have also realized there is no sense in confining their cooperation to smuggling people when the same systems and the same routes can be used to move heroin from China through Russia to Europe and the United States.

The Russian smuggling of human contraband is elaborate and well organized. Once the Chinese arrive in Moscow, they are housed in "hotels," dilapidated apartment buildings, usually on the outskirts of the city, where armed guards keep them in and everybody else out. The Chinese aliens are supplied with genuine passports that will allow them to exit Russia. These are often Russian passports or those from the former Soviet republic of Kazakhstan, whose citizens resemble Chinese. The Chinese will also need third-country entry visas, which are usually obtained from African countries like Libya, Liberia, and Somalia, though the Chinese have not the slightest intention of ever setting foot in those countries. U.S. visas can be a problem to obtain, but a problem that $10,000 is able to solve. For $10,000, illegals can buy a visa that has been expertly forged and is capable of fooling inspectors at ports all along the way until they get to New York, where they can make a phony claim for asylum that will tie the U.S. legal system up in knots for years. Alternatively, they can use the money to go to the Dominican Republic, where well-placed bribes are enough to get them through the airport and to the eastern coast to the wooden boats known as *yolas*, whose captains will ferry illegals to Puerto Rico and thus the United States for a very reasonable fee.

But before they are sent on their way, the illegals are, according to one Russian smuggler who spoke with the press on condition of anonymity, tutored in basic English. They don't learn the usual "Good morning" and "Pleased to meet you," but rather such useful phrases as "I was a part of the Tiananmen Square democracy movement," "We would like to raise a family, but China allows only one child per family," and "We have no human rights." The smuggler claimed a success rate of 80 to 90 percent for the graduates of his basic Berlitz/Cook's tour operation —30,000 of his illegals had slipped past America's gatekeepers.

After seventy years of pent-up criminal energy under the Soviets, the Russian gangs are entering every market, new and old, with vigor and cunning. They have even put their own new spin on the trade in human contraband. A Department of Justice intelligence assessment informs us that "trained assassins, imported from Siberia and Ukraine, allegedly hired by Italian organized crime, arrive on B1/B2 visas [intended for visiting businessmen] via Germany to commit contract murders in the United States and subsequently leave the country."

Many Russian criminals travel on visas and passports forged by former KGB officials whose previous responsibilities included supplying spies with documents that would pass inspection anywhere in the world. Moscow has also emerged as a major market for stolen passports, a subject to be discussed separately later in this chapter.

Last, the Russian Mafiyas have found yet another wrinkle to the human contraband business. In the past, Russians could enter the United States by the bushel load as long as they could claim a Jewish background or that they were political dissidents. With today's quotas for Russians down, it is far harder to emigrate to the United States legally. Sponsorship from America is thus a rare and valuable commodity. For a hefty fee, some Russian mafiosi promise all the necessary documents and then abscond with the money; for them, a simple swindle is less stressful than the actual transshipment of human cargo. If the mafiosi themselves want to travel to the United States, all they need is a legitimate business purpose and a legitimate American sponsor. Some Russians in the United States have import and export businesses that do little more than import Russians and export visa requests.

MEXICO

Cooperation between Russian and Chinese smuggling operations has been extended to include criminal organizations working in our hemisphere. On May 29, 1996, American authorities announced the breaking of the second smuggling ring within a period of six months, both of which were run by women. Gladys Garza Cantu, fifty-one, a native of Honduras and a naturalized American citizen, was arrested for smuggling Chinese, Indian, and Pakistani illegals into the United States—they had each paid in the vicinity of $28,000 in three disbursements to their handlers. Lodged in safe houses en route in Moscow, Havana, Managua, Guatemala, and Mexico City, they were transported in the final stages of their journey in a tractor-trailer modified to carry as many as a hundred people in a secret compartment. Ultimately, teenagers ferried the illegals across the Rio Grande in inner tubes to a muddy floodplain south of McAllen, Texas. Garza had been systematically bribing Mexican border and police officials, some of whom have also been arrested. Her business was netting her more than $1 million a year. The other woman gang leader, Peruvian-born Gloria Canales, was arrested in December 1995 in Honduras. She too had run a lucrative smuggling operation.

The publicity generated by the *Golden Venture* incident led to tightened security on maritime routes. Criminals are not only quick to spot new sources of revenue but also equally quick to alter their tactics as soon as law enforcement has uncovered them. Doris Meissner, commissioner of the Immigration and Naturalization Service, says: "We've stopped that illegal boat traffic, but there are still a lot of people coming from Asia, many through Central America and Mexico."

Most of the nearly 1 million Mexicans entering our country illegally are "local crossers," people living within a 50-mile radius of the U.S. border who cross over to work or to reside permanently, later bringing over the rest of their families. Living so close to the border, they tend to be familiar with the better crossing points and therefore have no need of the help of smugglers. "Long-distance crossers" are those who live more than 50 miles from the U.S. border; 95 percent of them are assisted by smugglers who are knowledgeable about U.S. immigration operations like Hold the Line and Gatekeeper and switch routes accordingly. What the Department of Justice calls OTMs (Other Than Mexicans) accounted for less than 2 percent of the crossers. But it is those who are, of course, the best-paying customers and are the primary concern of the criminal organizations. In addition to Asians, the principal OTMs are, in order of magnitude, nationals from El Salvador, Guatemala, Honduras, Nicaragua, and Ecuador.

Mexican authorities have been cooperative in the attempt to stem the flow of illegal immigrants across our southern border. Corruption remains the pivotal issue. The Mexican police official whom Garza had in her pocket received a salary of $400 a month. The bribe she was observed paying him was $9,200. In other words, he could make in an hour what it would otherwise take him twenty-three months to earn, an offer that may not be impossible to refuse but one that requires more moral grit than most people have.

Cuba and Others

Cubans attempting to reach this country illegally became a significant problem in 1994, when over 32,061 were interdicted by U.S. Coast Guard and Navy vessels. On September 9, 1994, an accord was signed by the Cuban and American governments allowing for at least 20,000 Cubans to enter the United States legally each year. For the time being that agreement seems to be effective in keeping the number of illegal Cuban immigrants at manageable levels. But it is worth taking a quick look at the past, at the background of these events, for it can serve us as a guide to potential dangers in the years to come.

Writing in the spring 1996 issue of *Trends in Organized Crime*, Alex Schmid and Ernesto Savona make the following observation about the well-publicized exodus of the Mariel boat people: ". . . between April and October 1980 . . . Fidel Castro was faced by 11,000 Cuban workers who sought to leave the country for Peru. He managed to redirect the refugee stream to the United States, diluting it with ten times as many others, including undesirables, mentally ill and criminals. Altogether, 124,779 Mariel refugees were used by Castro in what has been described as 'demographic warfare.' " In other words, the world's migratory populations not only are a source of revenue for criminal organizations but also can be used as a new instrument of state terrorism.

Other islands offer accessible launch points to our shores. Some of the Bahamas, a 750-mile arc of 700 islands, only 29 of which are inhabited, lie only 50 miles from the southeast coast of Florida, making them a convenient site for smuggling into the United States. Depending on the type of vessel used and sea conditions, smugglers can usually reach the Florida coast in not much more than an hour. Working both day and night, guided by Florida's coastline lights, speedboats carrying up to thirty passengers are used to deliver illegal aliens to this country—Haitians, Cubans, Dominicans, Guyanese, Turks, Indians, Pakistanis, and Chinese nationals. Many Bahamian rings that formerly engaged in the smuggling of cocaine and marijuana are now believed to have switched to the human contraband trade, no doubt because of the low-risk, high-gain factor.

The Dominican Republic, which lies 77 miles from the west coast of Puerto Rico, is also a favored launch point for smugglers. Nationals from China, Cuba, and the former Yugoslavia have been apprehended while attempting to enter the United States illegally, usually in *yolas*, although high-speed craft are also used. The Dominican Republic suffers from a 30 percent unemployment rate, which means that many of those being smuggled are Dominicans. Judging by apprehensions, Jamaica is also a major transit point for Chinese, Indians, Pakistanis, Sri Lankans, and Bangladeshis.

Illegal immigration is driven by a push-pull factor. The push is political or religious oppression, onerous government policies (the one-child edict in China), human rights violations, and the lack of educational opportunities. The pull, by far the greater force in most cases, is the lure of America and other developed countries, which afford the economic opportunities unavailable at home. The dislocation and migration of large numbers of people is one of the megatrends of this unsettled time. It will continue to prove a lucrative field for those who deal in human contraband as long as the chance for gain remains so high and the risk so low.

Your Papers, Please

Just as money laundering is an inevitable corollary of the narcotics traffic, the trade in human contraband could not exist without forged documents or genuine ones illegally obtained. Except for the Mexican workers who dart across the border to earn a day's pay and then return home, every illegal alien sooner or later will need papers of one sort or another. Though we have stressed the large number of aliens who enter this country by foot and by ship, not to mention those floating across the Rio Grande in inner tubes, it should not be forgotten that significant numbers arrive here by air and must therefore be supplied with high-quality passports, visas, and other such documents able to pass inspection.

Here once again modern technology is put to the service of criminal intent. Laser printers, computer imaging, and enhancing technology can produce both $100 bills and travel documents that can deceive the unwary. The Nigerians have carved out a niche for themselves in the false documentation business, though they are hardly alone. Chinese nationals have been intercepted entering Canada with counterfeit Korean passports. Jamaicans are adept at altering British passports, and Poles, no longer routinely granted asylum after the fall of communism, frequently enter this country with high-quality page- or photo-substituted passports. Haitians use fraudulent documentation— for example, a Florida birth registration card and personal identification card purchased for $5,000—when traveling by air to Florida, avoiding airports such as Nassau and Freeport where the

U.S. Immigration and Naturalization Service conducts preflight inspections.

Next to the Chinese, the Dominicans are the largest group of "inadmissibles." This group employs the greatest variety of fraudulent documentation, including photo-substituted Dominican passports, genuine Dominican passports containing counterfeit U.S. nonimmigrant visas, fraudulent birth certificates, and alien registration cards. Smuggling organizations strike deals with Dominicans who have become naturalized U.S. citizens to apply for passports, which the smugglers buy and which the holder then reports lost or stolen. Dominican criminal organizations have forged links with the Chinese triads, selling them Dominican passports for $21,000 for subsequent use by Chinese nationals. And, as we have mentioned, many former officials of the KGB and other East European intelligence agencies who once counterfeited documents as part of their jobs have now found a more remunerative market for their skills in the "private market" of crime.

Russia has emerged as one of the principal centers of the human contraband trade for a host of reasons. Its geography makes it an obvious transit point for Chinese, Indian, and Pakistani migrants traveling westward to Europe and the United States. Aeroflot and the other Russian airlines offer highly competitive prices, though their safety standards and safety records are abysmal. Passport control is both lax and corrupt. Russian border guards and passport control officials are responsible only for verifying the authenticity of Russian passports and exit visas. They are not responsible for verifying the authenticity of foreign passports and visas. If a traveler has a valid Russian entry visa, that person is entitled to board a flight and enter the country. Even that limited control system does not appear to function with any particular efficacy. A Russian security minister has stated that in the second half of 1993, 240,000 foreigners left Russia for whom there was no record that they had ever entered the country in the first place.

The cause of that "inefficiency" is corruption, which is rife and often comes at a laughably low cost—a package of cigarettes and a few dollars can solve nearly every problem connected with irregularities in documentation. The tough old seasoned veterans of Russian border control have been replaced by younger people who still receive Soviet-era salaries and who, serving a state that does not have the old regime's political will to safeguard the inviolability of its borders, are particularly susceptible to bribery.

Moscow has also emerged as a major market for stolen passports. These are of two sorts: blank, unissued passports stolen from passport-issuing agencies around the world, and those stolen from groups of tourists in hotels or from travel agencies. In times of turmoil, passports are also looted from issuing agencies, as took place in 1995 in Liberia when a significant number disappeared from the American consulate. Those documents are then sold to smuggling organizations and suitably altered. According to a U.S. Department of Justice strategic assessment entitled *The Use of Moscow by Transit Migrants to Access the West:* "Russian Customs officials have seized numerous Federal Express packages containing recycled fraudulent documents and altered passports sent from the United States. These packages were addressed to various Chinese, Indian, Somali and other nationalities scattered throughout Moscow."

On June 28, 1993, in Milan, Italy, three Chinese nationals were arrested with stolen Polish passports. Seven thousand blank, unissued Polish passports were known to have been stolen, and further investigation proved that these had been among them. Despite claims that the passports had been obtained in Warsaw, subsequent examination of the entry and exit stamps revealed that they had been obtained in Moscow. Polish passports are particularly desirable because Polish citizens can enter most Western European countries without a visa.

Russian criminal organizations specializing in the smuggling of human contraband are as savvy about the legal and illegal routes and points of entry into Western Europe as the Mexicans are about the Rio Grande and other points along the southern border of the United States. Though the cheapest means of travel from China to Moscow is by land, the most frequent route used by illegal Chinese emigrants is from China to Moscow by air, then to Spain by land. They then fly with forged documents from Madrid to the United States. Some illegals are smuggled across the Russian border with Norway. In 1992 a Somali smuggling route was uncovered that led from Kiev to Murmansk, then on to the Norwegian border. These illegals had obtained Russian visas in Ukraine through bribery. Trawlers and freighters are used to smuggle Iraqi Kurds from Russia and the Baltic republics into Sweden at a price of $2,000 per head.

The Czech Republic has also emerged as a major transit point for illegals from China and the former Yugoslavia. This leg of the journey tends to cost less—between $63 and $95 to cross the Slovakian and Hungarian borders, and up to $254 to pass into Germany, a more desirable destination.

Some illegals remain in Europe, causing the same problems there as they do in this country, chiefly an overburdening of social service systems and an increase in the crime rate by those stranded without funds and livelihood who cannot repay exorbitant smuggling charges. The fiscal stress suffered by the governments and citizens of California, South Florida, and New York will soon extend to other states just as surely as the narcotics epidemic spread from the big cities to the small towns of this country.

Illegals poison the political atmosphere for legal immigrants. In the United States, they have been responsible for increasingly punitive laws against all immigrants, laws that would deny immigrant children schooling and health care. We must continue to refuse to punish those who come to the United States legally, and separate them from those who come in uninvited and in violation of our laws. But we must also be much more tough-minded regarding the illegals. Although children, whoever they are, must be educated, fed, and housed while they are here, if illegal they must all be sent back, along with the rest of their families, to the land from which they have come; that is the only means of protecting the legal immigration system and our law itself. And if that country refuses to take them, we should recognize that as the hostile action that it is, and prepare that country to face a proportionate loss of access to our country in return.

In this light it is interesting to see that China continues to take back illegal emigrants from the United States, at some cost, even when U.S.-Chinese relations are otherwise tenuous. We have not had a foreign policy crisis over immigration yet, but that does not mean we could not have one in the very near future.

But, severe as it may be, the problem is not solely budgetary. The systematic violation of a country's borders and the counterfeiting of its passports and other identification documents are an assault on sovereignty and yet another factor contributing to the "climate of ungovernability." Historically, many wars began with border incidents, one country probing the protective membrane of another. In the war with the transnational criminal organizations, our borders are flouted regularly, whether by smugglers carrying narcotics or trading in the most precious and pathetic commodity of all—human beings.

8

Where the Dirty Money Washes Up

WHY ROB A BANK if you can own one?" This wisecrack is attributed to Rafik Svo, an Armenian crime lord who in early July 1993 convened a summit in Yerevan, the country's capital, for serious deliberation of a serious subject—how to turn Russia's new banking system into a money-laundering operation that would dwarf any other.

But there's some wisdom in that wisecrack in that it mirrors perfectly the new criminal mentality. Although transnational crime organizations do indeed mimic modern corporations in many ways, the differences, ultimately, are more essential. It is not only that such organizations routinely use murder as an instrument of competition; what truly defines and distinguishes them is that their main problem is not making a profit but using that profit freely in the public economy. The final law that must be broken in the criminal process is what might be called the illegal legitimization of their profit, or, as it is usually known, money laundering.

"Laundering" is the perfect word. The money is dirty, bloodstained. And copious beyond measure.

Money laundering, estimated to run close to $500 billion a year, has been called the third largest business in the world, right after currency exchange and car production. Though always a criminal act, it is not always performed by professional criminals. It attracts the full spectrum of citizens—everyone from divorcing spouses hiding income and companies "shielding" profit to governments performing covert actions. Corporations wishing to bribe foreign officials also need to cover their trail: Twenty years ago Gulf Oil is known to have laundered $4 million through the Bahamas to cover its payoffs to Korean and Bolivian politicians; Lockheed Corporation moved $25.5 million through a Liechtenstein trust en route to Italian politicians, to take but two of the larger examples. The banks and other financial systems that engage in money laundering could not care less whether their client is Gulf, Oliver North, Colonel Muammar el-Qaddafi, or the Cali cartel.

Willie Sutton robbed banks because "that's where the money was." Modern transnationals prefer to own banks because that's where the money can be freed up for use. Russia was in an ideal position to instantly become a major player in this field, as the wisecracking Mr. Svo was well aware. The new free Russia was just forming its first real banking system. Compared to the heydays of the KGB, the state was relatively toothless. Officials could be bribed, uncooperative bankers could be simply slain. In short order, more than half of the banks founded in the five years since the fall of communism have been in mob hands.

Bad enough in itself, criminal ownership and/or control of such vital institutions as banks is by its nature damage that cannot be contained. Contamination of the banking system cannot be sustained without corruption of the legislature. In some countries, like, most notoriously, the Seychelles, the criminals are themselves writing the laws that suit them best—or, to be more precise, their lawyers are. Furthermore, laundering funds through a mob-run business rather than through a bank nearly always has a deleterious effect on the competition. The mob's video rental store or construction company is happy to break even. Yours has got to make a real profit.

Moving and legitimizing their income is a constant preoccupation for all transnational criminal organizations. Part, though not all, of the problem is the elephantine amounts of sheer cash involved. Five million dollars in $100 bills weighs over 125 pounds, and billions in cash must be moved. However, a good deal of criminal income—for example, the hundreds of millions made each year through fraud—is electronic from the start. But even those electrons are dirty and must move with stealth into the financial system.

The ploys range from the crudest to the most sophisticated. Just as cocaine is smuggled into this country in condoms that are swallowed, cash is smuggled back out in the same way, with both male and female smugglers exploiting their bodies in grotesque ways. A common ruse favored for a time in South Africa was to have a passenger appear at an airport with his leg in a cast and request a wheelchair to take him on board the plane. Meanwhile, an anonymous phone tip had alerted authorities that the man's cast concealed an illegally large amount of hard currency. Naturally, this led to a confrontation with the authorities. Naturally, the man was outraged and summoned both his lawyer and the press, but in the end he succumbed to the pressure and allowed the cast to be removed. Naturally, it was empty. He threatened a lawsuit—not only had he missed his plane but he had been subject to gross indignities. Naturally, the airline was all apologies. When the passenger appeared the next day with his new cast, he was ushered onto the plane with the maximum of graciousness, and needless to say, that cast was now lined with crisp hundreds.

The tricks and dodges are legion. When governments like the United States enact laws requiring people to report movements of currency worth $10,000 or more whenever they cross national borders, the criminals squeeze the water out of the bills to make them weigh less, and ship them in bulk through the U.S. Postal Service, Federal Express, or DHL for placement in banks outside the United States.

When I learned of this practice during my investigations in 1988, I insisted that U.S. laws require major money-laundering countries to adopt laws similar to ours on reporting currency, or to face sanctions if they didn't. Panama and Venezuela wound up negotiating what were called Kerry Agreements with the United States and became less vulnerable to the placement of U.S. currency by drug traffickers in the process. Indeed, today, the Clinton administration is taking the Kerry Agreement idea one step further—advising what President Clinton calls "egregious money-laundering centers" that if they don't change their ways, the United States will take appropriate, proportionate responses of an economic nature to make these centers feel our pain. Administration officials tell me that the very hint of such an approach by the United States has already pushed several countries in the Caribbean and Western Europe to begin imposing real regulations to combat the launderers.

Regardless of the methods used, money laundering is driven by a common set of needs and considerations. In a lively, thorough, and valuable recent book on the subject, *The Laundrymen*, author Jeffrey Robinson spells them out with admirable clarity:

> There are four factors common to all money laundering operations. First, the ownership and source of the money must be concealed. . . . Next, the form it takes must be changed. No one wants to wash $3 million in $20 bills only to wind up with $3 million in $20 bills. Changing the form also means reducing the bulk. Contrary to popular belief, you cannot stuff $1 million into an attaché case. . . . Third, the trail left by the process must be obscured. The whole purpose of money laundering is defeated if someone can follow the money from beginning to end. Finally, constant control must be maintained over the process. After all, many of the people who come into the picture while the money is being laundered know that it is dirty money, and if they steal it, there's little the original owner can legally do about it.

Robinson's list of the basic needs of the launderers is complete. However, those shopping for ways and means to clean their money have a long list of requirements and criteria. They prefer countries that engage in a high volume of interbank transfers, maintain rigid bank secrecy, require minimal or no identification to conduct financial transactions, offer ease of incorporation, and have established access to international bullion trading centers in New York, Istanbul, Zurich, Dubai, and Bombay. They are also attracted by countries that import or export significant amounts of gems, especially diamonds—countries where the dollar is readily acceptable as currency and whose law-enforcement agencies have limited asset seizure or confiscation capability.

There are plenty to choose from. The world of money laundering is as varied and multicultural as the world of crime itself, as the world we live in. Competition is fierce. Some organizations are centuries old, such as the Chinese and Indian systems of forwarding funds. In these systems, money changers receive deposits and, through a loose arrangement with other money changers, hand out cash on the basis of chits. Apart from the chits, there are no records kept and no way to determine what the original source of the money was. Other systems have a lineage of mere months, like the mushrooming banks of today's turbulent and corrupt Russia. Nearly every country in the world is involved. The U.S. Department of State, Bureau for International Narcotics and Law Enforcement Affairs, publishes an annual *International Narcotics Control Strategy Report*, the most recent issued in March 1997. Aside from assessing the narcotics situation in every country, the report devotes the last hundred of its 598 pages to a similar review of money laundering, rating each of more than 190 countries in terms of significance from Aruba (high) to Zambia (low).

Here, however, it is necessary to focus on a sampling of representative countries and cases, a real approximation of the range and variety of means and institutions involved, starting with the sunny Caribbean and ending in the snows of Russia.

Where?

RECENTLY, a certain foreign intelligence service had a remarkable opportunity. A certain bank on a certain Caribbean island was being shut down for money laundering, and the intelligence service was given the weekend to check out the records before the police officially arrived.

As the intelligence agent who went into the bank later told me, he found a treasure trove of information—records of accounts of some of the world's most powerful leaders. "If the people of those countries had any idea of what their leaders were up to, they'd revolt," the intelligence agent remarked, and

I agreed. But they would never know. The bank accounts had been selected for their secrecy, and that secrecy was not something the foreign intelligence service was in any position to break.

By design, most of the nearly 900,000 visitors to Grand Cayman each year never see the island's powerful offshore financial center. It is an invisible business, protected by official secrecy written into Caymanian law. But it has transformed this sliver of coral, sand, and rock 250 miles due south of the Florida Keys into a moneymaking machine, the most successful of the world's offshore banking tax havens.

The capital city of George Town is small and still almost quaint in spite of the glut of boutiques; visitors can walk its commercial center end to end in five minutes and never suspect that billions of dollars are at work here. Some 533 banks are licensed in these few square blocks, and 29,298 companies are registered, but most are little more than a brass nameplate on an office wall, a computer, and a phone line. More than $420 billion in assets is held here, over $15 million for every man, woman, and child in the country. But there are no tellers or security vaults; today money is electronic, and it can move from George Town through Guernsey to Hong Kong at a keystroke.

Too frequently it is dirty money. Investment banker Dennis Levine visited George Town to set up an account just before his arrest. In 1985 and 1986, Oliver North used a Caymanian company to front the arms-for-hostages swap. Pakistani banker Agha Hasan Abedi, the mastermind behind BCCI, used a Caymanian subsidiary to hide for some fifteen years the improper loans he used to buy Washington's First American Bank. The offshore banks of the Cayman Islands and other postage-stamp-sized havens are where criminal money trails end, cloaked by legal secrecy; they are a bolt hole for tax evaders and a safe haven for swindlers, embezzlers, and crooked S&L owners, as well as a Laundromat for drug dealers, who fly in with Halliburton suitcases filled with $100 bills.

Today, some sixty offshore financial centers, mostly small sovereignties with fewer people than a small town and no economic base, permit foreigners to engage in financial transactions using the country as a base, so long as the transactions are entirely offshore. In essence, what this means is that they provide no-tax, no-regulation licenses to engage in financial and business transactions to anyone who wants them. Such havens are used by large corporations to reduce the taxes they owe large countries like the United States. But they are also used by anyone with something to hide, since money that leaves an offshore haven has no reason to resemble—in amount, type, or ownership—the money that entered the haven.

Although few Americans even know offshore centers exist, offshore banking is booming: George Town's assets have doubled in size during the 1990s; internationally, 50 percent of the world's illegal economic activity flows through these havens, and $5 trillion in assets is held offshore. Tiny countries in the Caribbean, the English Channel, and the South Pacific now routinely defraud the United States and other countries of tens of billions in tax dollars by providing the crooked with offshore asylums for their money in secret shell corporations and hidden trusts. The Internal Revenue Service, the FBI, the State Department, and police forces around the world are almost powerless to stop them.

Offshore banking today is a sophisticated and segmented business. Cyprus serves Eastern Europe and the Russian Mafiya; Chinese crime lords most often bank in Hong Kong, Singapore, or Vanuatu. Switzerland still has the best reputation for probity, although it has been losing market share since tightening regulation and relaxing secrecy. Drug dealers favor Antigua and Aruba at the moment, but they move from haven to haven across the Caribbean, creating ever more complicated schemes to outwit international law enforcement.

Wherever they are located, however, tax havens are engaged in piracy; they are stealing the assets of other countries. There is no reason for money to be in the Caymans or any other haven except tax evasion, money laundering, or fraud. It is all accommodated, but not without consequences. Once illegal money moves to a country, corruption follows like day the night. The crime lords begin to build political power to protect their money. Soon they control not only the financial system, but the legal and political institutions as well. In fact, they are only taking logical steps to protect their interests—ill intent is irrelevant.

Using the Panamanian banks, dictator Manuel Noriega

created a civil regime indistinguishable from a global criminal gang, where the state and its bankers sponsored drug and arms trafficking and prostitution, as well as engaging in money laundering and tax evasion. Before the American invasion Noriega was on the payrolls of the Colombian drug cartels (among many such organizations), Israeli arms traffickers and assassins, and an array of intelligence agencies, including our own CIA. Noriega was a big believer in equal opportunity.

The dictator's main financial partner, the then little-known $23 billion Bank of Credit and Commerce International (BCCI), was equally criminal, as my investigation first uncovered in 1988 and proved three years later when the bank was shut down globally through the simultaneous action of bank regulators. BCCI was at the heart of the Islamic nuclear bomb program in Pakistan; credit financier for the U.S. TOW missiles shipped to Iran during the Iran-Contra affair; money-mover for the CIA, the KGB, the PLO, terrorist Abu Nidal, Saddam Hussein, and a number of infamous weapons dealers. Fueled by the profits from global crime, the bank spread corruption worldwide, putting government officials from Zimbabwe, Nigeria, Venezuela, Panama, China, Saudi Arabia, and even the United Kingdom on its payroll.

Noriega was not, unfortunately, an isolated case. As the prime minister of the former British colony of St. Kitts and Nevis admitted in 1996, his country faces the possibility of winding up totally controlled by drug traffickers. In September 1995 a large shipment of cocaine to the sons of the deputy prime minister ended up with two of them being arrested and a third being murdered in a mob hit; later the island's senior criminal investigator was murdered while probing the crime. St. Kitts was left near anarchy. Things continued to worsen in late 1996, when a local judge inexplicably released from jail three major drug traffickers wanted by the United States, giving them back all of their seized assets. During the trial the traffickers were joking and laughing, and days before the judge entered his decision their friends, who apparently felt secure in the outcome, held a victory party for them. Senior U.S. government officials warn that Antigua, Dominica, and many other Caribbean islands are similarly threatened.

Nations that are willing to rent themselves to money

launderers too often are willing to sell citizenships as well. After all, if you are willing to take the criminals' money, why not accept the criminals themselves? *The Economist* regularly runs ads for intriguing anonymous services, and in 1994 my staff sent for the brochures. One such brochure made the following proposition: "We can offer completely legal acknowledged citizenship, naturalization, including travel documents, driver's license, ID card from different countries which are UNO [United Nations Organization] members. Prices start from U.S. $17,900 for a computer-registered passport from the Dominican Republic up to U.S. $19,900 for a Panama citizenship." As of today, you can purchase citizenships from St. Lucia and Dominica in the Caribbean by Internet, on-line, for similar prices. Citizenship in Ireland is offered, too, but at premium prices of $50,000 and up, under Irish economic citizenship programs designed to bring much-needed revenue to a chronically undercapitalized European nation.

Even sovereignty and citizenship are for sale if you know how to shop around.

Heroin in New York, Diamonds in Hong Kong, Cash in China

CHINA

The Chinese diaspora, plus the existence of four Chinas —the People's Republic, Hong Kong, Taiwan, and Macao—is especially amenable to money laundering. In fact, the Chinese scattered worldwide have for centuries made use of private remittance systems to move money. Based on trust, those systems predate the Chinese commercial banking and postal systems, but are still favored by many legitimate businesses. Needless to say, they are ideal for criminals. A DEA intelligence division report, *Asian Money Movement Methods*, notes the advantages of the UBS (underground banking system):

Use of the UBS has several advantages over the official banking system, the first being *anonymity*. Although ledgers are kept and receipts are given to the remitters, UBS systems create no official paper trails, a priority for those moving illegal funds or avoiding taxes.

The system is also *faster* than the official banks. Hundreds of thousands of U.S. dollars can be transferred in a matter of a few hours, if necessary. Banks, on the other hand, are notorious for holding money transfers or "taking their time" in clearing checks, which enables them to earn interest on the money they are holding.

The *low cost* is a third advantage. Chinese underground bankers charge only a small fee because their profit is made in exploiting "unofficial" currency exchange rates, which are more favorable than banks' official exchange rates.

The triads also use precious gems—diamonds, rubies, emeralds—to launder money. They sell heroin in the United States and buy diamonds in the jewelry center of New York's Chinatown. The diamonds are then sent by courier to Hong Kong, which requires no reporting on their import. And the cherry on top is that those diamonds can be sold at a nice profit in glamorous, diamond-starved Hong Kong.

By contrast, the bulk smuggling of currency remains the principal means for moving drug money into China itself. Why? Because the corrupt communist system encourages people to bring in as much hard currency as they can carry—as long as they declare it, no further questions are asked.

MEXICO

Mexico's long border with the American Southwest makes it an ideal route for not only the smuggling of narcotics and illegal aliens into the United States but the smuggling of cash proceeds back out as well. In April 1995, $6 million in cash was discovered hidden inside a shipment of air conditioners; in October, troops of Mexico's 13th military zone seized a Cessna 210 aircraft containing $12 million near the city of Tepic in the state of Nayarit. But the shipments of cash are only part of the problem.

According to the U.S. State Department, Mexico has become the "money laundering haven of choice for initial placement of U.S. drug cash into the world's financial system . . . Mexican officials have estimated that the amount of drug cash being repatriated to Mexican drug cartels in 1994 was some $30 billion and the total amount moved into Mexico for eventual repatriation to Colombia is much higher."

Though Mexico has laws against money laundering, they have proved largely ineffective for the obvious reason—a slice of the staggering amounts of money moving through the system is used to bribe officials, from bankers to government leaders. And some of those officials not only sanction the practice of money laundering for a price but also engage in it themselves.

From 1988 to 1994, when his brother Carlos Salinas was president of Mexico, Raúl Salinas de Gotari transferred $80 million to $90 million from a Citibank branch in Mexico City through Citibank headquarters in New York to a Swiss bank account. Citibank also moved some of the money into dummy corporations in the Cayman Islands. Raúl Salinas received a government salary of $190,000 a year and had no known activities as a businessman. He is suspected of connections with the narcotics cartels, though those allegations remain as yet unproved. Currently in a maximum security prison, Salinas has been officially accused of financial crimes and conspiracy to commit murder. Motives for the murder, the assassination of his brother-in-law Ruiz Massieu, who was then Mexico's chief prosecutor responsible for investigating the murder of Carlos Salinas's handpicked successor for Mexico's presidency, remain murky. Was it personal revenge, a family killing, a consequence of a financial deal, or part of a cover-up? The theories grew only wilder in October 1996 when a human skeleton was found buried on property owned by Raúl Salinas, at a spot predicted by a Mexican psychic.

"How could anyone named Salinas using his own name deposit millions of dollars without questions being raised?" asked Ronald K. Noble, a former under secretary of the Treasury who now heads an international task force on money laundering. The answer, according to *The New York Times* of June 5, 1996, is: "The instructions from Citibank's New York headquarters to clerks at the bank's Mexico City office were clear: Ask no questions." Salinas, a man fond of living high and marrying beautiful women, offered another explanation, in a volume of verse he published in 1990:

> *If you rob from many 100 percent*
> *There could be a moral offense.*
> *A few points more, a few points less*
> *Morality is a question of percent.*

RUSSIA

The joke about owning banks instead of robbing them was based on the very practical consideration that in the years after the fall of communism a bank cost less than a Mercedes. In Soviet Russia, the prisoners of the Gulag, known as *zeks*, referred to their camps as the Zone and the rest of the country as the Big Zone, meaning the whole damn thing was one big Gulag. But all that changed when the red flag came down from the Kremlin on December 25, 1991. A new Zone was created, a shadow zone where crime, government, and business merge.

What kind of people were drawn to the new Zone? They include felon Grigori Loutchansky, whom *Time* magazine has called probably "the world's most investigated man." Western intelligence services say point-blank that Loutchansky has engaged in major money laundering. Reviews of his business records in Zurich confirmed this to a Western European journalist, who shared his experience with the U.S. government. But beyond the allegations of his firm's money laundering is an intriguing, if elusive, story of shadowy links to governments and intelligence agencies for Loutchansky and his partners. A decade ago this fifty-one-year-old Georgian-born Russian was doing time in a Latvian prison for black-market activities. Released from jail through the help of the KGB, Loutchansky was then set up with Communist Party funds to run a new multinational trading firm, Nordex, based in Vienna. By 1993, Nordex wound up with a monopoly on Ukrainian oil imports, even as Loutchansky consolidated his power through developing relationships with key Russian politicians like former deputy prime minister Vladimir Shcherbakov and Prime Minister Viktor Chernomyrdin. Fueled by KGB funds, Nordex mushroomed to become a multibillion-dollar operation within three years of its founding, developing relationships with the heads of government in key former Soviet states like Ukraine, Latvia, and Kazakhstan; with the sons of the late British media tycoon Robert Maxwell; and with key political figures in Israel to boot. The keys to the firm's success are access and a willingness to ignore the ordinary rules that govern more conventionally founded businesses. Is Loutchansky a criminal? An apparatchik? An intelligence agent? A businessman? Loutchansky and Nordex have consistently denied any involvement in criminal activity, claiming only that he has a knack for being in the right place at the right time, for putting deals together to help important politicians like former Ukrainian president Leonid Kravchuk, and for meeting such prominent people as U.S. president Bill Clinton. Loutchansky denies publicly that he trades in nuclear arms, in prostitution, or with the Mafiya. But media reports paint a different story, describing Loutchansky as not only a mobster and businessman but also a key member of the new Russian elite, with links to the ruling elites that stretch all the way to Austria and Israel.

Until July 19, 1995, the new elite included forty-year-old banker Oleg Kantor, president of the Yugorsky Bank, founded in 1991 but already one of the largest banks in Russia. Kantor was a key player in a 3-trillion-ruble oil- and gas-lending syndicate —a man of mysteries, it was said, who kept all his secrets in his head, a powerful member of Russia's politically powerful oil and gas lobby, which in June 1995 threw its weight behind a center-right political bloc set up by Prime Minister Chernomyrdin to contest parliamentary elections in December. Then on July 19, Kantor met the fate of a growing number of members of Russia's new elite: He was murdered, together with his bodyguard, outside the luxury hotel where he leased two floors. Kantor was knifed seventeen times, his throat slit, his chest slashed vertically in half. Kantor's murder followed some forty-six assassinations of prominent Russians in Moscow during the first half of 1995, with ninety-five more murders attempted, and not a single case solved by the authorities. The Kantor murder was merely the latest in a series of mob hits of top bankers, prompting the head of Russia's Association of Bankers to call the murder another attempt by organized crime to seize control of a bank.

The money the Russian mobs want to launder comes more from economic crime than from narcotics dealing or human contraband. The main activity of the mobs is stripping the country of its resources. According to the economic crime unit of the MVD (the Ministry of Internal Affairs), by 1994, economic crime had become one of the largest industries in Russia, surpassing in size and importance branches of the national economy such as construction, timber, pulp and paper, chemicals and petrochemicals, and ferrous metallurgy. The MVD calculated that each of these industries represented less than 5 percent of Russia's gross domestic product, whereas losses from economic crime overall well exceeded 5 percent of Russia's GDP.

In some industries, like oil exports, losses to crime totaled 20 percent of the total Russian gross domestic product. In the area of fertilizer exports, Russian law enforcement estimates that 34 percent of the total fertilizer available for export is stolen. The Russian Academy of Sciences estimated in 1995 that as much as 60 percent of Russian capital has already moved into the hands of criminal structures, which control as much as 85 percent of the voting stock of Russian corporations and 50 to 80 percent of all banks. But the Mafiya, though controlling those banks, has no illusions about their security or permanence. The dirty money doesn't stay there long.

Swiss officials have acknowledged that between 1992 and 1995 some $54 billion was deposited in Swiss banks from Russia. All those profits, as well as the revenues from criminal activities as traditionally defined, had to be laundered. And while they were at it, the Russian mafiosi decided to become launderers to the world. In record time they had replaced Panama as the center for cleaning money for the Colombian cartels and the Italian Mafia. Now we see just how far the new Shadow Zone extends, because this entire new venture might well have foundered except for the unwitting cooperation of the Republic National Bank of New York and the U.S. Federal Reserve.

Five nights a week Delta Flight 30 leaves New York for Moscow, carrying in its hold more than a ton of crisp $100s fresh from the mint, amounting to $100 million. An estimated $40 billion has been shipped to Russia in this way since January 1994, an amount greatly in excess of the total value of all Russian rubles in circulation. The Treasury is happy—it makes $99.96 from every bill that is never presented in the United States for payment (4 cents is the printing cost). The Fed "passes the buck" to Republic, the bank actually supplying the Russian banks with the bills. "What do we know of Republic's customers?" said New York Fed spokesman Peter Bakstansky. "We don't. It's their responsibility to know who they are sending it to." Republic too pleads ignorance. "That's my responsibility, to make sure we don't sell to the banks that have organized-crime ties," said Richard Annicharico, a retired FBI agent and now one of Republic's officials in charge of compliance with money-laundering regulations. "That's the hardest thing to find. In fact, if you know of any, let me know."

Meanwhile, the money continues to flow into Moscow at the rate of at least $500 million a week. Security on the flights is surprisingly light, given the amounts of cool cash involved. But as a Mafiya source told *New York* magazine for its cover story "The Money Plane": "If you rip off Russian banks, you rip off the Russian mob. And no one's got big enough balls or a small enough brain to do that."

The Russian banking situation could not be more murky, exactly the way the mob wants it to stay. Felons can own banks, and Russia still has no laws about money laundering. Jonathan Winer, of the State Department's Bureau for International Narcotics and Law Enforcement Affairs, put it like this after a September 1995 meeting in Moscow with Viktor Melnikov, the Central Bank's director for foreign currency control: "It's very difficult to tell from the outside what a transaction [with a Russian bank] really means. There are not a lot of public documents. You can't go to an SEC to look at the balance sheet for a Russian firm the way you can in the United States. You can't go to a bank regulator and [find out] what kinds of loans have been made, what the underlying source of capital is, or any other number of key issues, let alone who their customers are. These are issues which the Russian Central Bank is concerned about. These are issues which the Russian Association of Bankers is concerned about, because they are not unrelated to the murder of the bankers."

The control of the Russian banks by the Mafiya perfectly

illustrates three of the chief features of contemporary organized crime:

1. It will corrupt the specific financial or business system in which it operates.

2. That corruption will inevitably taint other systems in the society, including the executive branch of government, the courts, the legislature, other business sectors, even the media. In the Seychelles, the mob itself writes the banking laws. In Colombia, the segment of the construction industry under cartel control for the purposes of laundering money has already driven legitimate competitors out of business simply by underpricing them. In Russia, the Mafiya attempts to influence everything from government to the press to business. Relationships between government officials, major industrial firms, banks, the media, and known gangsters are so intermingled that, as one former Russian parliamentarian told me, you cannot say where any of these institutions begins or ends. In important respects, the Mafiyas and the government merge.

3. That corruption will not be confined to its country of origin. As we have seen, the corrupt Russian banks launder money not only for domestic criminals but for the Italian Mafia and the Colombian cartels as well. The Italian, Colombian, and Russian money that is laundered is reinvested, in turn, in legitimate businesses, from construction to pharmaceuticals, as well as in buying politicians. In Russia, parliamentarians are given immunity from all prosecution, so several mafiosi have used their money to get themselves elected to the Russian Duma, a safe haven from which they can extend their power beyond the borders of Russia.

And, perhaps most ominously, the Russian transnational criminal organizations appear to have now set their sights even on trying to suborn Israel's social and political system.

Under the Law of Return, Israel will accept anyone who is Jewish, whether that person is from Ethiopia or Vladivostok. In the last twenty years many Russian-Jewish criminals were among those flooding to the United States and Israel. Under the Soviets, being a Jew was considered a nationality and was registered on the internal passport every Soviet citizen had to carry and present on demand. Soviets with one Jewish parent and one

Russian parent had the choice of which nationality they preferred to be listed as. Because of the rampant anti-Semitism in Russia many, of course, preferred to be registered as Russians.

With the opening of emigration to Israel and the United States, the situation was suddenly reversed and large numbers of people wanted the Russian listing to be changed to Jewish. And a good many weren't Jewish at all, but "became" so because it looked as if it could pay.

The reasons were simple. Israel already had a large Russian-speaking population, money laundering was not against the law, and the weather, compared to Moscow's, was ideal.

In 1996 the U.S. State Department upped its rating of Israel as a money-laundering center from medium to medium-high, reflecting public statements by senior Israeli officials that Israel was emerging as a more significant money-laundering center for Russian criminals.

Israeli officials have stated that Israeli organized crime has processed drug proceeds through Israeli financial institutions, in Israel and abroad, using U.S. dollars. Banking laws designed to attract foreign capital, a policy of not taxing foreign accounts, and an active but not fully regulated stock exchange continue to make Israel an attractive investment and financial safe haven.

In September 1996 senior Israeli officials revealed to the Israeli press that they had uncovered a ring of Russian criminals who had illegally acquired Israeli citizenship. These criminals included some of the most notorious mobsters in Moscow, representing several organizations considered by Western intelligence to be among those of greatest global concern. Not only had these criminals become Israeli citizens and moved to Tel Aviv, but they also had been buying property, such as hotels, in Israel, and some of them even seemed interested in financing Israeli political parties.

As Israel prepared to deport these criminals, Israeli officials were acknowledging that for the first time in its history Israel was under a different kind of threat than that posed by Palestinians denying the right of Israel to exist. This threat was more insidious. As Israeli interior (police) minister Moshe Shahal publicly warned, these Russian mobsters were attempting to directly infiltrate businesses and political parties in Israel for the purpose of creating a safe haven for themselves there.

This shocking development is requiring Israel to consider a variety of steps, from the basic—passing laws to discourage money laundering—to the profound, such as considering amendments to the Law of Return to prevent criminals from entering Israel, whether they be genuine Jews or "counterfeit" ones. In the end, the money-laundering problem becomes a genuine threat to Israel's fundamental identity and basic security, a threat from inside the country rather than from Israel's historic enemies.

Given its special nature, Israel is a particularly painful example of how transnational criminals inevitably erode a nation's sovereignty, jeopardize its security, and even threaten its very sense and definition of identity.

Money laundering is sometimes described as a victimless crime. We would be fools to believe it.

9

A Vision of Victory

CORPORATIONS, communications, crime—everything's gone global, everything but the response of law, our sole defense against a Darwinian world of murder and money.

It was a great moment in our civilization, a moment celebrated by the Greek playwrights, when we switched from the law of vengeance to the rule of law. But the rule of law must be rewon again each day. Eternal vigilance *is* the price of liberty.

None of us can feel secure so long as each faces the risk, at any moment, of becoming a victim of random crime, whether it's a drive-by shooting or financial fraud. What all international crimes have in common is that they create unintended victims as well as intended ones. Alien smugglers, car thieves, drug traffickers, terrorists, and fraudsters do not care whose lives and well-being they threaten. Their target is all of us: family, community, businesses, financial systems, political institutions.

To emerge victorious in the war against global crime, what we really need is at the very least the two basic things the bad guys have—first, an international network of reliable partners; second, the resources to do the job.

In part, solving the second issue provides a key to solving the first. While some new resources will have to be committed, what is needed is not just new sources of funding for the United States or any other government. Much of the money to fight crime already exists—it is just that the criminals control it rather than the governments. The governments need to grab those resources back, and there is a way to do that without taxes or bribes, as we'll discuss.

But to deal with transnational criminals, a far more profound change is needed. We need nothing less than a revolution in the way we conceive of every aspect of the law, from jurisdiction to punishment. More precisely, we find ourselves in a position where we are compelled by the globalization of crime to globalize law and law enforcement.

That does not mean that we substitute the United Nations or any other kind of global body for protecting ourselves under our domestic laws and with domestic police, domestic prosecutions, and domestic courts according to our own Constitution. To the contrary, security starts at home, in the community, with community-based law-enforcement institutions that work. There is no substitute for having a cop on the beat who knows his community, has sources there, and can step in to deal with trouble as it happens. Nor does it mean restricting our ability to act in our own interest by submitting to an international entity outside our control.

But countries must be willing to work with other countries across borders to deal with criminals. We need to move beyond traditional notions of national sovereignty when those traditional notions benefit only the bad guys.

Today, the most significant, ever-present threats to the national sovereignty of most countries are not foreign invasions, foreign subversion, or foreign military actions. Those threats have not disappeared, as Saddam Hussein proved more than six years ago when he invaded Kuwait, and as the fighting in Bosnia and various parts of Africa in recent years has demonstrated. But literally every day, the national sovereignty of the United States and every other country is violated by the criminals who ignore our borders and laws, and invade our waters and territory carrying out illegal activities that cost our citizens billions of dollars and thousands of lives. Yet it is outdated, often contrived sovereignty issues that too often prevent effective cooperation.

Today, when a Dominican hit man comes to the United States and engages in a contract killing that winds up also taking the lives of innocent bystanders in the process, if he can reach Dominican soil before the United States grabs him, he is home scot-free. He will not be prosecuted in the Dominican Republic, nor will he be extradited to the United States. The same is true if he is Panamanian, Costa Rican, Russian, or, for all practical purposes, French.

Today, when a Colombian drug trafficker in a Honduran-flagged boat enters French or Dutch waters at either end of the Caribbean island of St. Martin, he knows the U.S. Coast Guard vessel that has been pursuing him will have to stop at the three-mile limit, the traditional outer limit of territorial waters. He'll be free to unload his illegal cargo, while the United States goes through the complex process of getting permission to follow from the relevant government.

In both cases, it is the criminals who are taking advantage of national sovereignty to conduct their criminal enterprises, and the governments and the citizens whose security those governments were created to protect who are being violated by their own reluctance to respond.

In a globalized world, our national security is only as strong as the weakest link. Yet the weak links are almost everywhere. Border controls in Eastern Europe, the former Soviet Union, and much of Southeast Asia are practically nonexistent. While criminals cross borders, police authority stops at every border. A crime defined one way in one country has a different definition in another, and with no international criminal code, criminals exploit these differences. Police in many countries cannot use such tools of surveillance as a bug or even binoculars against mafia operatives. France refuses to extradite its criminals even for the most serious offenses, preferring in theory to try them in France, but in practice providing too many of them with safe haven. Neighboring Holland, a major drug transit zone, has had minimal drug-law enforcement within its borders. As a result, in early 1996, French-Dutch relations temporarily collapsed, with French prime minister Jacques Chirac and Dutch prime minister Wim Kok trading accusations about which country was more responsible for the European drug problem. Canada still permits anyone to come into the country with briefcases stuffed with cash, no declarations required, no questions asked. In the Caribbean, major traffickers go free because there is no ability to protect witnesses. After twenty-two witnesses were murdered in Trinidad in 1995, criminal prosecutions of major drug cases essentially stopped because of the inability to get anyone still alive to talk. In Vienna, Austrian banks continue to offer anonymous bank accounts to any Austrian citizen, who is free to sell that account to the local Russian mobster or anyone else, a situation that so offended the European Union, of which Austria is a member, that the EU has decided to sue Austria over the practice.

Our domestic defenses are not much better. Our chief federal law-enforcement agencies, the DEA and the FBI, have too often been rivals rather than allies in suppressing the drug trade, failing to share information with each other or with the federal prosecutors for whom they theoretically work. Our chief information-gathering agencies, the CIA and the National Security Agency, have too often been unable to share usable information with law enforcement because to do so would endanger their sources or their technologies, or both. Worse, even when they do provide information, law-enforcement agencies often shrug their shoulders, turning up their noses at information that hasn't been generated by one of their own wiretaps or snitches.

Criminals can pick and choose how and where they want to commit their crimes, and which jurisdictions are most likely to offer them protection. Meanwhile, at every level of enforcement, from the coast guard to customs, from local police to U.S. attorneys' offices, from the Immigration and Naturalization Service to the Bureau of Alcohol, Tobacco and Firearms, our methods of capturing and prosecuting criminals are better suited to petty thieves than high-tech drug cartels and arms-smuggling rings—not to mention international bank fraud and money laundering, with its bewildering paper and e-mail trails in dozens of languages.

We simply must recognize that the world's patchwork quilt of legal systems is as much an anachronism as carbon paper. A working system of laws to combat transnational crime must be hammered out among nations of good will. For example, we have a million Salvadorians in the United States. A small number of them commit crimes against other Salvadorians here, then return to El Salvador. We have no extradition agreement with El Salvador because such a law was not written into its constitution. Neither does its law allow it to try Salvadorians in El Salvador for crimes committed in our country. Criminals are often considerably less intelligent than their devilishly sinister screen incarnations would suggest, but you don't have to be a genius to take advantage of easy travel and safe havens.

But the Salvadorian example is relatively simple. How do you make a case against a person who plans a crime in New York City against British nationals living in Guatemala, when the crime is committed by Panamanians? Who is going to prosecute that crime? The Brits can't do it because nothing has happened in Britain. The United States can't do it because no one was hurt here. The Guatemalans don't have the capacity and the Panamanians have no interest in it.

Testifying before my subcommittee, Jack A. Blum, a lawyer who specializes in international criminal law, put it this way:

> The movie *Bonnie and Clyde* has a scene in which the pair waves goodbye to the Oklahoma state police as they cross the line into Texas. As a result of the experience of the 1930s, when interstate movement of criminals increased, the United States began to develop criminal law at the federal level. For the first time the federal government began to run national law enforcement agencies that could follow the criminals wherever they went. The agencies could also cooperate with, and coordinate, the activities of state and local jurisdictions. Today, the world law enforcement system is where the United States was in the 1920s.

So our greatest single task is to articulate and achieve a new international convention that totally overhauls our ability to jointly investigate, move evidence, secure witnesses, and, most important, help build adequate legal institutions in other countries. A world moving toward a seamless web of commerce cannot protect itself without enforceable law and standards that are almost equally as seamless. Just as we developed new rules of the road as commerce expanded contacts between the growing states of the United States, so now we must break barriers and build stronger cooperative arrangements internationally.

We must aggressively move into a new realm of foreign assistance to build up judicial systems incorporating common standards and procedures. It is entirely to the benefit of law-abiding nations to do so, yet many in Congress resist such efforts based on short-term and shortsighted monetary rationales. Public diplomacy must assume a much larger role in this mission, helping to define the problem and promoting solutions, a task well suited to USIA and our leadership abilities. Instead of closing outposts or consulates abroad, we should be expanding our diplomatic effort significantly. The leader of the free world should not be retrenching in the opening rounds of the post–Cold War match. It is ironic that despite universal acceptance of the complexities presented by globalization and technology and the critical need to assert our interests abroad, we are nickel-and-diming these very efforts.

When a foreign national is arrested here, we must consider importing the criminal law of that person's country and applying it in the United States, so that we can prosecute to the fullest in one location. Given the multiple geographical connections of most modern crimes, this step may be our only way of giving law enforcement adequate punch. We do this today in civil cases under choice-of-law rules, and rather than witness international jurisdictional gridlock, which results in a crime going unpunished, we should strive for reasonable practicality.

Achieving this will not put any of our rights or interests at risk. On the contrary, not to do this is to continue to put us at risk. Increasing power accruing to offshore financial havens undermines the legitimate tax base of our nation, while exposing our entire financial system to the potential of massive fraud or unexpected setback.

Obviously, the United States cannot go it alone. Mighty as we are, the war against crime and terrorism can be prosecuted successfully only in alliance with many other nations. If a criminal can target an American citizen, business, or institution and then find safe haven in another country, his home will literally be his castle and the rest of us no more than peasants. That means we have to face facts and recognize reality when a nation decides to go over to the other side and become the partner in crime, or at least a sidekick, of the criminal. We have to recognize in the area of crime, just as we have in terrorism, that there are such things as "state sponsors of criminality"—some by intention, others by neglect. In the same way we have, as policy required, worked to isolate state sponsors of terrorism, we must be prepared to isolate state sponsors of criminality. In the same way we have tried to strengthen the political will of states of uncertain commitment to fighting terrorism, we must strengthen the will of states whose commitment to fighting crime remains uncertain. In the same way we have enlisted the world's press in condemning terrorist actions, we must place the damage caused by transnational crime before the world media so that the world's peoples can see it and respond appropriately.

A normal state is one with the will, desire, and resources to cooperate in the struggle against global crime. Obviously, developed countries such as Britain, France, Germany, Italy, and Japan are vigorous in the pursuit of criminals and to some degree inclined to cooperate in building an international legal network, though local political needs and passions always muddy the waters. In others, like Russia and China, where corruption is rife, the results are more mixed, yet these countries can be worked with, and must be. Failed states are those which, like Haiti or Lebanon, may have the will and desire to combat crime but simply lack the resources. A criminal state like Myanmar or Noriega's Panama is one in which the government is actively involved in activities that are criminal by common international consent.

The three types of states reflect a three-stage process of criminalization that Paul Stares in his book *Global Habit: The Drug Problem in a Borderless World* defines as follows:

> . . . trafficking groups evolve from an initial predatory stage, in which small-scale gangs seize control of particular businesses or turf, to the parasitical stage, whereby the state's institutions, public officials, and infrastructure become routinely corrupted and exploited for their ends, to the final symbiotic stage, in which the interests of organized crime and the state essentially coalesce to the extent that the line between licit and illicit activities becomes so blurred as to be meaningless.

Criminal states need to be isolated and forced to reform, through limiting their access to the benefits of globalization. There is no good reason to make it easy for people from such countries to travel to other countries or to facilitate business in their countries. We consistently stood up to the Soviet Union until it collapsed. We, along with others in the international community, banned business in South Africa until it abandoned the illicit racialism of apartheid and accepted democracy for all. A semi-criminalized dictatorship like the SLORC of Myanmar or the Nigerian military has as its first victims its own people. But its criminality also threatens to undermine its neighbors and its region, even as it claims victims globally. Such regimes should not be treated with respect by other nations, but should be instead subject to limitations on travel, investment, and access to the most developed nations until such time as they take sufficient steps to justify re-admittance to the community of nations.

The same kind of approach would be fully justified were it determined that one nation was involved in counterfeiting the currency of another and using that counterfeit currency to finance its own operations. We may soon face this last situation. U.S. government officials have acknowledged that they are investigating the issue of state sponsorship in connection with the manufacture of the so-called supernote, a counterfeit U.S. $100 bill that is very difficult to distinguish from the real thing. No nation has yet been named as the perpetrator, but some experts believe only states have sufficient expertise to manufacture a note of such quality. The intentional counterfeiting of another country's currency, an action considered by Adolf Hitler against the United Kingdom during World War II but never carried out, is certainly an act of extraordinary belligerence—some might argue an act of war—and should be responded to accordingly. What response is appropriate depends on the danger posed by the threat and what is necessary to respond, as we shall discuss shortly.

States that have been corrupted, or are incompetent, need a different approach. In such states, many officials, as well as most ordinary citizens, have a profound desire to see their country fight off the criminals. The job there is to identify the people and institutions who want to do the right thing and find ways to help them to do it. For instance, when a drug trafficker is moving narcotics by boat, he may have bribed customs officials at a port, but if local police know the shipment is in town, they can alert the coast guard from another country to intercept the boat in international waters. With teamwork, good people can beat out the bad.

What's clear, however, is that interdiction, even with the best cooperation by many states, cannot stop the illicit trades alone. In the war against global crimes, interdiction, whether of heroin, plutonium, or smuggled illegal immigrants, is usually just an annoyance to the enemy. When I served in Vietnam, one of our missions was to stop the flow of arms from the north. Though we were often successful, the overall movement of arms was never seriously impeded. Likewise, we will never be able to stanch the flow of criminal products and services merely by going after it in transit. Reengineering international law requires us to recognize that not only must criminals, small and large, be apprehended, but also their systems must be attacked at the vital choke points. And that means going after what motivates all criminal activity in the first place—the money.

Seize and Share

As of now, the criminals have the money and governments do not. So, the first secret to victory in the war against transnational crime is to seize and share the criminals' assets.

No country can be reasonably expected to assist us in our struggle with crime if it does not see direct benefit for itself, especially if it is among the countries with highly limited funds for law enforcement, which include a great many nations these days.

We absolutely must push for asset forfeiture laws all over the planet. In the words of one plainspoken lawman, "Get their ass and get their assets." Our intelligence and law-enforcement agencies, in cooperation with those of other nations, can gather information to target the businesses and the business assets of the criminals. That information serves as the basis for seizure orders. The assets are arrested at the same time as the suspect.

But it is not enough to seize the assets; they must be shared creatively. Countries must be rewarded for their cooperation. And what better place to derive those proceeds than from the ill-gotten gains of the transnationals? It's only poetic justice.

Between 1989 and December 1995 the international asset-sharing program resulted in the forfeiture in the United States of a little less than $125 million ($124,679,340.22, to be exact to the penny). Over $40 million was shared with foreign governments that had cooperated in the investigations. In 1995 the Department of Justice, which administers the program, transferred almost $4 million to Ecuador, a little over $2 million to Switzerland, and a half million dollars to the United Kingdom; other countries like Canada and Israel received smaller amounts, $41,418 and $34,770, respectively. In 1995 the United States reached an asset-sharing agreement with Mexico and a similar reciprocal-sharing agreement with Canada. So far, asset sharing has been pretty much a one-way street, with only Switzerland, the Isle of Jersey, and the United Kingdom having shared forfeited assets with the United States.

Asset seizure, however, also has a dark and dangerous underside, one which is now no secret. In fact, it was front-page news in *The New York Times* of March 19, 1996, which, in an article entitled "When Drug Kingpins Fall, Illicit Assets Buy a Cushion," identified the problem: ". . . defendants are often able to negotiate lighter sentences by offering to lead prosecutors to property hidden around the world, or by promising not to put up lengthy court challenges to the forfeitures . . . defendants who have succeeded at crime can essentially buy down their sentences, while those who have never made it big have no bargaining chips."

To let the rich buy off their crimes is morally wrong. We must ensure that asset forfeitures do not become a substitute for serving time. Similar discretion needs to be used in dealing with informers, who should never be permitted to avoid lengthy sentences when they themselves have committed offenses that shock the conscience. Whenever U.S. prosecutors suggest that informants and plea bargains are an effective way of going after the kingpins, their counterparts in other countries remind them of the risk of abuse of plea bargains. Indeed, Colombia is a perfect example of the failure of the plea-bargain system. The notorious kings of cocaine, the Ochoa brothers, kept all their assets and each served just five years in prison.

The situation is rife with possibilities for subtle corruption. The Justice Department is now taking in half a billion dollars a year in forfeitures, a significant portion of which is shared with state and local law-enforcement agencies—some of which rely on such money for as much as 10 percent of their budgets. Since crime is now transnational, it is no surprise that the personal holdings of the criminals themselves are often located in any number of foreign lands—yachts in the Caribbean, homes in the south of France, and all the other accoutrements of immense personal fortune. As Supreme Court Associate Justice John Paul Stevens has written with admirable understatement: ". . . it is not unthinkable that a wealthy defendant might bargain for a light sentence by voluntarily 'forfeiting' property to which the Government has no statutory entitlement. This, of course, is not the law."

A better balance needs to be struck here. On the one hand, it is simply a mockery of justice if criminals are rewarded for their success by essentially buying themselves lighter time; on the other hand, a stiff sentence that leaves the vast wealth they have amassed in their control, for the use of their family, friends, and associates, does not sit right either. The seizure and forfeiture of assets acquired by criminal means is too valuable and effective a weapon in the war against crime to allow its strength to be dissipated through misuse.

Some basic principles need to be agreed upon by the world's wealthiest nations, like the G-7 (which is composed of Canada, France, Germany, Italy, Japan, the United Kingdom, and the United States), and exported to the rest of the world.

Start from the premise that big-league criminals should not be permitted to keep the proceeds of their crimes, regardless of where these proceeds have been invested. Add to that the agreement that ownership of financial assets must be transparent to law enforcement: Every country should create systematic recordkeeping requirements for financial and real property and allow these records to be shared in cases involving serious crime. Add in procedural safeguards to ensure a public hearing process before seized assets can be forfeited to the government. Encourage smaller governments to share information whenever a big-time crook uses their jurisdiction, and provide quick rewards through asset sharing. Take them together, and you go some distance to shifting the balance of forces from the bad guys toward the cops.

Shame, Shame, Shame

OBVIOUSLY, asset seizure and sharing can be a very powerful instrument and inducement, but it is not going to appeal to what we have termed "criminal states" or "sovereignties for sale." Such states will perceive no interest in seizing criminal assets. On the contrary, their very existence is predicated on the protection of such assets. What do we do about them?

The answer is that if the dangled carrot of asset sharing fails to produce results, we switch to the stick. We prohibit American companies from doing any business with known foreign-based criminal enterprises or their fronts. We refuse anyone associated with those organizations the right to travel to the United States, do business here, or use any of our institutions, banks, etc. Moreover, we must go after their dirty money, closing down the offshore financial centers that shelter and launder criminal profits. Experts estimate that the drug traffickers alone launder a quarter of a trillion dollars a year, money they then use to take over legitimate businesses. The dozen or so countries that exist only to launder and shelter money must be made to desist. We have the power: We could refuse to allow pirate financiers to repatriate U.S. currency, or impose customs limitations on their trade and search all their cargoes, or forbid Americans to do business in these countries, much as they are now forbidden to trade in the outlaw states of Cuba, Iraq, and North Korea.

In the truly egregious cases, where we have evidence that a state has fully gone over to the side of the criminals, we are locked in a state of belligerence, if not indeed at war. Such states are never democratic. Instead, they have sold their governance for a few pieces of silver and can no longer purport to represent their peoples. Are we justified in such cases in engaging in economic warfare as a means of reprisal? We are. But if we try to do so alone, we run the risk of victimizing ourselves rather than our intended targets. Here, too, going it alone is not a solution. We must build a multilateral front to be most effective.

Cracking down on the worst offshore bankers is just part of the solution, however. We must convince the rest of the international community to act with us, ensuring that their nationals don't trade in dirty offshore finance, and that their own domestic banks are regulated and open to inspection. Bank secrecy is a tradition in many of our sovereign allies; it is the key to Luxembourg's prosperity, and written into the Austrian constitution. For such countries, we must insist on the kind of controls contained in the U.S.-Swiss agreement of 1977. Long notorious as a haven for any kind of suspect funds, Switzerland is now cooperating significantly with international law-enforcement efforts and breaking down its walls of secrecy where they stand in the way of legitimate investigations or standards.

We must also insist that the movement of capital electronically be regulated far more strictly, to keep global crime lords from moving their gains at will. Today a Dominican in Miami can send his profits virtually anywhere in the world via something as mundane as an American Express Moneygram, and complicated laundering schemes need only one cooperative banker to bundle dirty money in a larger wire transfer.

As put forth by the Basel Convention, which governs international banking standards, all banks of signatory countries (all major industrialized nations) are obligated to "know their customer" before opening accounts and engaging in banking transactions. If the standards by which banks accept money were lived up to with the same diligence as that by which most banks lend money, the "know your customer" maxim would have teeth. But too many bankers pretend they are doing all they can to know what money crosses their threshold and pretend they are not as key as they are to law-enforcement efforts. Competition and the extraordinary sums of money at stake distort the behavior of players at every level!

The technology is already available to monitor all electronic money transfers. We need the will to make sure it is put in place.

We can make sure that economic interests controlled or

owned by criminals are declared threats and forced out of business as President Clinton did with Colombia in his executive Order 12978 on "Blocking Assets and Prohibiting Transactions with Significant Narcotics Traffickers," in which he asserted "that the actions of significant foreign narcotics traffickers centered in Colombia, and the unparalleled violence, corruption, and harm that they cause in the United States and abroad, constitute an unusual and extraordinary threat to the national security, foreign policy, and economy of the United States," and declared "a national emergency to deal with that threat."

Strategies

IN THE WAR AGAINST international crime and terrorism, we need a revolution in legal concepts, multiple alliances, and a three-pronged strategy: multilateral, bilateral, and unilateral.

MULTILATERAL. We must lead the effort to build an entirely new, multilateral code of behavior—international standards to deal with criminal activity—that we are committed to enforce so as to isolate noncomplying countries and institutions. That is fundamentally how the Western world defied and stood up to the communist threat. We worked to isolate communist nations economically. We began with containment and then fought them militarily, until to everyone's surprise and delight they collapsed under the strain.

In daily practice, a multilateral strategy means building a web of human relationships—cop to cop, judge to judge, diplomat to diplomat, intelligence analyst to intelligence analyst— that is united by a set of common concerns. Those relationships must transcend individual cases and go on for years. To build these relationships will require nothing less than a full and deliberate commitment by every legitimate government to making the rule of civilized law the dominant force on the planet.

BILATERAL. While working for global law and order, America must attend first to strengthening its immediate relationships with allies on law-enforcement matters. We already exchange practical law-enforcement information on a daily basis with countries like the G-7 nations. We have mutual legal assistance arrangements with dozens of additional countries to permit our courts to recognize one another's evidence for trials. We now need to consider experimenting with our closest partners in a system that sets up special courts to try cases at home involving victims abroad. In such cases, which would be accepted only by agreement between both nations, trials could take place wherever the evidence and witnesses were located, applying the laws of the country where the crime took place.

Let's imagine how such a system might work in a case involving a French national who has ordered a contract killing of an American in Thailand by an Italian as a result of a failed heroin deal. Today, only Thailand would be able to prosecute such a case. At best, the Italian hit man would be the only person likely to face trial; getting the Italian courts to extradite him could take years, and the likelihood of his French boss being in turn extradited would be even more remote. Under the "special court" system, the United States, whose citizen was the victim and therefore might have the greatest interest in a prosecution, could take charge of the investigation, seek to extradite the Frenchman and the Italian at the same time, and apply the murder laws of Thailand in a trial at a special court in Washington. If convicted, the Frenchman and the Italian could then either serve their sentences in the United States or be returned to serve time at home. Either way, the chances of justice being served would be substantially increased over the current situation.

UNILATERAL. In dealing with states that are outright criminal, the United States may at times need to take unilateral action to protect its citizens, its interests, its integrity. This need not take as dramatic a form as our invasion of Panama and arrest of General Manuel Noriega, though it would be unwise in dealing with criminal states to rule out that option a priori. It does mean that we can and should punish countries that willfully refuse to protect our citizens and in effect become state sponsors of criminality, as we are now doing with Myanmar and Nigeria.

The United States has not only sanctioned Nigeria for its failure to cooperate against narcotics, making it ineligible for U.S.-supported international lending, but has shut down direct flights from Nigeria to the United States, making it harder for Nigerian criminals to gain access to our country. In the meantime, U.S. diplomats and law-enforcement agents have coordinated a multinational strategy of criticism directed at Nigeria for its failure to combat business frauds (many of which emanate from telephones installed at Nigerian government offices!). These steps need to be bolstered by additional measures, such as treating all transactions involving Nigerian banks as "suspicious," and requiring U.S. financial institutions to report such transactions to law enforcement. This kind of "Scarlet Letter" would be the mark of Cain for any country, and have a very substantial impact on the ability of its nationals to do business internationally. Care needs to be exercised in taking these kinds of steps precisely because they are so effective.

An important and complicated country like China necessitates a range of strategic approaches. Clearly, we have to continue working with its judiciary and law-enforcement officials who have a genuine interest in combating international crime, a problem they know will become only more acute when mainland China inherits the triads of Hong Kong at the stroke of midnight on June 30, 1997. We must continue to build relationships with people who want to do the right thing but have barely begun.

But we must also utilize the power of exposure and public embarrassment. No state in the world can sustain public attention to the issue of corruption. It is not often mentioned, but as I learned from my discussions in Beijing, those who rose against communist rule on Tiananmen Square, especially the working people, were moved as much by a revulsion against corruption as a fervor for democracy.

Stiffer penalties can be imposed on countries that do not respond either to offers of cooperation or to their public shaming for corruption. It can be made more difficult for those countries to access U.S. markets. We can grab assets—and freeze them—as we have done in the past. When our citizens were held hostage in 1980, we froze the assets of the Ayatollah in Iran. Thirteen years later we froze the assets of the Haitian junta. We have also frozen the assets of terrorists and the Cali cartel. We didn't just order American businesses not to deal with such outlaws, we threatened to freeze their assets as well if they disregarded the directives of the law.

Sharing the Assets
of Expertise and Intelligence

EVEN IF the United States had ten times the money it now possesses for combating international crime and terrorism, it would not be sufficient. Other values must be recognized and shared, chief among them expertise and intelligence. The task before us is daunting and intricate, as was made painfully clear by the June 1996 terrorist attack on the American compound in Dhahran, Saudi Arabia. We had requested that the terrorists arrested for an attack in Riyadh in November 1995 that killed five Americans be interrogated so that more could be learned about the terrorists' organizational structure and intentions, with the obvious hope of preventing the sort of incident that later occurred. For a host of reasons, the Saudis preferred to punish the terrorists quickly—by beheading them, no surer way imaginable of rendering them uncommunicative. The barrier of cultural differences and perceived political necessities prevented a more reasonable approach that would have been in the best interest of both us and the Saudis. Result—death, destruction, destabilization.

But even those barriers can be made to fall by the skillful application of appropriate political pressures and financial inducements coupled with programs for sharing methodology and information. The director of the FBI, Louis J. Freeh, in a report of May 31, 1996, entitled *The FBI's Presence Overseas*, stated the problem as follows:

> If the FBI operates only in the United States, there is no way that we can cope with crime threats of foreign origin that suddenly arrive full-blown in the United States.
> But a small, super-efficient system of FBI Agents abroad working with their police counterparts in many countries can provide assistance and information to the FBI at home that can be obtained in no other way. . . . If we are forced to act alone, restricted to our own borders, we will be easier targets for foreign criminals.

At the present time, seventy senior FBI special agents are working in twenty-three nations, helping to deal with the volume of international criminal cases, whose number more than doubled between 1984 and 1993. These agents are, as a rule, accredited as diplomats in the countries to which they are assigned and work from offices in the American Embassy in tandem with the authorities of the host country. Those offices are known as legal attaché offices, legats in FBI parlance. Depending on the country, the agents' activities cover a broad spectrum—facilitating the flow of information between the United States and the host country, getting involved in specific investigations, training and technical assistance. In fiscal 1995 the FBI's overseas offices handled more than 11,000 matters, but as Director Freeh stresses, the agents are "*not* intelligence officers; they are *not* a shadow intelligence agency; and they will *not* engage in espionage. They are law enforcement agents—dedicated to fighting organized crime, terrorism, violent crime, drug trafficking, and economic crime."

Though recent in inception and still limited in scope, the legat program has already scored some impressive successes. The Italian government's attack on the Mafia, spearheaded by Judge Giovanni Falcone, received considerable aid from Legat Rome, which secured testimony and evidence from witnesses in the United States. In turn, the federal prosecution of the major Mafia crime families in the northeastern United States could not have succeeded to the extent it did without the extensive cooperation of the Italian police and investigating magistrates, with Judge Falcone again playing a leading role.

Legat Moscow, officially opened on July 4, 1994, has worked closely with the Russian Ministry of Internal Affairs (MVD). That cooperation was instrumental in the arrest of Vyacheslav Ivankov, known as Yaponchik ("Little Japanese"), considered the most important Russian organized crime figure in the United States. Legat Moscow played a pivotal role in the March 1995 arrest in the United Kingdom of a St. Petersburg gang that had penetrated the computers of a major bank in New York and transferred $10 million to dummy accounts. In November 1994, Legat Moscow, working with the Russian authorities, uncovered an illicit shipment of $250 million in diamonds en route to San Francisco.

New legats are opening in such places as Warsaw, Cairo, Tel Aviv, and Islamabad, Pakistan, with others still being negotiated in places like Riyadh and Beijing.

The legat system is working, but it is only a bare-bones beginning. Seventy agents, no matter how "superefficient," are insufficient, given the size of the enemy's ranks.

In addition to the FBI, we have agents based around the world representing U.S. Customs, our immigration service, our Drug Enforcement Administration, our Secret Service, our coast guard, and even our Internal Revenue Service. Altogether, some two thousand U.S. law-enforcement agents are now based outside the United States at our missions around the world, acting as liaisons between local law-enforcement agencies and U.S. federal law enforcement.

But even this veritable army of foreign cops can handle only a fraction of the cases referred to them. Moreover, few of them are today supervised by anyone. Instead, they are left alone in the field with little guidance, often acting as little more than mail drops and liaisons between governments, given little ability to actually direct or guide investigations.

We can do better than that. In 1994, I went to President Clinton and we agreed it was essential to put 100,000 more cops on U.S. streets within five years. We were told by others in Congress that the resources were not there and that we were dreaming, but ultimately we did cut other parts of government in order to find the money for the 100,000.

Today, with rising tax revenues from the longest economic recovery in our history and a national deficit of just 1.5 percent —the lowest in the developed world—the United States can certainly afford to add another thousand U.S. law-enforcement officials around the world to be our advance guard against transnational crime. Our additional thousand agents must not be just cops. They must include prosecutors, trainers, legal specialists, and diplomats who recognize law enforcement as a national security problem and are ready to deal with it as part of the routine of their daily work. Every U.S. embassy in the world should have a law-enforcement team, with every ambassador recognizing that a portion of his job is to make sure our foreign policy promotes law-enforcement interests. Even today, too many ambassadors think that law-enforcement is for the cops only. In truth, an ambassador cannot promote American business, cannot protect American citizens, cannot promote democracy, without understanding the role that crime and law enforcement play in the country to which he or she is accredited.

Sacrifice

THE NATIONS of the earth that stand for the rule of civilized law must be willing to make sacrifices if that rule is to endure. While none of us is willing—nor should we be—to give up any sovereignty, we must reexamine and, if necessary, change some laws to harmonize with a new, effective system of international law and punishment. Rethinking sovereignty should not mean less local control or less local responsibility for law enforcement. It means finding ways to bridge national borders through the creation of minimum standards, which all nations must achieve.

Nations must agree both on a consistent system of laws and a consistent system of punishment. As matters now stand, money laundering is not a crime in Turkey or Russia, extradition is constitutionally banned in Colombia, and illicit financial dealings still account for too much of the business of banking systems in countries like Switzerland and Austria. A Haitian finds little to fear in an American penal system that provides dental care, educational facilities, and three meals a day. In Colombia, drug lords have found complete accommodations in their prison cells, enjoying large-screen televisions, mistresses, and reduced risk of getting killed in a turf war from inside. Walls do not a prison make, and unless the criminals face sufficient risks, and sufficient punishments, with no safe havens, they will continue to wager a life of crime as a good bet.

Some point to Singapore's draconian laws—the death penalty for narcotics traffickers, flogging for vandals—as the model for how to create a relatively crime-free society. But Singapore is not crime-free; although its streets are safe it is a major entrepôt for the shipping of illegal goods, and some of its banks harbor funds from numerous criminal organizations. The sophisticated managers of global crime don't need to worry about Singapore's death penalty; they will never set foot there.

The world community recognized the need for an international police information clearinghouse even before World War I, when INTERPOL's predecessor was established in Vienna. Today's INTERPOL was created after World War II. It provides state-of-the-art analysis of counterfeit currencies and false travel documents. And its databases on wanted criminals provide an important information-exchange mechanism for police forces all over the world. But INTERPOL is open to essentially every UN member nation, including those that are compromised. Its security has been breached over and over again by crime lords. And INTERPOL does nothing more than exchange information—it does not house a single "globo-cop" with the power to investigate. Every investigation that takes place of any crime anywhere in the world is still done by the police of one country or another.

We face two stark alternatives in responding to this problem: either we create a new kind of global supercop with the ability to investigate across borders, or we accept much broader notions of what is known in international law as extraterritoriality. The risks of creating a team of global supercops are obvious: Who would guard the guardians? How could such a team be simultaneously responsible for living within the laws and rules of individual countries? Wouldn't this truly be giving up our national sovereignties in a way that our people would be bound to find offensive and unacceptable?

The European Union has already faced this question over the past four years, during which it has tried, and failed, to create a EUROPOL with jurisdiction to investigate crimes throughout Europe. Led by the United Kingdom, country after country in Europe has pulled back from the idea of joint investigative activity through a regional body. Indeed, in some cases, European cooperation against crime has actually taken a step backward because of the anxieties raised by making crime fighting a European mission rather than a national one.

In truth, the idea of creating a team of global supercops is not just unworkable. It is a genuinely bad idea.

This leaves only one reasonable alternative: that nations expand their national legal jurisdiction to create a much broader ability to investigate and prosecute cases involving their citizens when the injuries take place beyond their shores.

The United States has already moved to some extraterritorial jurisdiction over crimes when they involve terrorism. The FBI will investigate, and the Justice Department will prosecute, terrorists abroad when they plan and commit crimes against Americans. The same kind of jurisdiction has not, however, been extended to other serious crimes. When Oklahoma businessman Paul Tatum was murdered in Moscow on November 3, 1996, family members and members of the American business community asked the United States to investigate, especially since many of them believed Russian officials were behind the murder. The United States found that it had no jurisdictional authority to investigate. There is no statute that today lets American law-enforcement officials take action simply because an American is murdered abroad. That kind of gap in jurisdiction made sense at a time when most people stayed in their home country most of the time, and when the costs and time of travel made it practically impossible to expect any governments to investigate events taking place outside their borders. This is a gap we can, and must, fill today. We cannot protect the Paul Tatums of the world if our police are deprived of the right to investigate, even in a situation when all affected countries agree such an investigation should take place and can be closely monitored to prevent abuse.

Obviously, this kind of expanded jurisdiction has to be used wisely. You do not want people expending enormous resources investigating cases they can't solve. You also do not want extraterritorial jurisdiction to create grave tensions among nations. But should the power to jointly investigate anywhere exist? It must.

Going abroad is not the only solution, of course. We need to get our own house in order. Legislators must join the executive and judicial branches of government in revising the laws and reconfiguring the relevant agencies to strengthen our response to the complex, multidimensional nature of global crime today.

Equally important, we need to end the turf wars, bureaucratic squabbling, and general confusion that characterize our fight against the global crime lords. The staffs of the relevant agencies take themselves and their internal affairs seriously enough; sadly, crime fighting itself often comes in a poor second. We need to bring about the same sort of reforms in these agencies that we see being urged on private corporations—reforms focused on results, not on the preservation of internal functions, bailiwicks, and status.

In September 1995, prodded by my subcommittee, the CIA agreed to include the investigation and infiltration of global criminal gangs as part of its mission. We must encourage intelligence agencies of other nations to do likewise—and to share what they find out. Cooperation, not competition, must be the guiding principle. Here again, some of our traditional notions about the clear distinctions among business, crime, and terrorism must be modified to fit the blurred realities of the new era.

A State Department paper of December 1994 entitled *Combating Transnational Crime: A Proposed Presidential Initiative* notes:

> Any credible international counter-crime initiative must optimize interaction between the intelligence and law enforcement communities. . . . State must continue to oversee this relationship from an intelligence angle to help resolve interagency disputes, manage the "gray area" between law enforcement and intelligence, and promote necessary intelligence hand-offs between foreign policy and intelligence or investigative agencies and departments. As our law enforcement–related activities increase overseas, sensitive intelligence on foreign law enforcement or criminal activities will grow. Deeper engagement could bring information on corrupt activities with foreign governments and companies. Such intelligence might, for example, suggest the need to restrict, change, or enhance our relationships with foreign contacts for political reasons—even though law enforcement cooperation might dictate otherwise. Law enforcement activities can have potentially significant foreign policy impact and must be weighed against other non-law-enforcement-related activities State may have in the national security domain.

Governments must also work together to develop new technologies to defeat the crime lords. The German government, for example, is now developing a system that enables the owner of a car that has been stolen to immobilize it electronically, from any distance. Spread throughout Europe, such a system would cripple the lucrative stolen car trade, one of the Russian Mafiya's favorite crimes. Another example: U.S. insurers already maintain a database of all cars stolen in this country. That database, coupled with treaties covering stolen vehicles, needs to be expanded globally so that criminals can no longer escape merely by moving a vehicle across a national border.

Other technologies must be pressed into service to create improvements in currencies—like the new U.S. $100 bill, strange as it still looks—and passports to prevent their counterfeiting. Communication and encryption devices must not be permitted to benefit cybercriminals and cyberterrorists to the detriment of the law abiding. In some cases, small but not onerous sacrifices by businesses and private individuals will be required.

Some people think a clipper chip can make it possible for law-enforcement agencies with warrants to intercept electronic communications when authorized by a judge. Others believe such technofixes can readily be circumvented by canny crooks. Similarly, some believe you can control the availability of encryption techniques in the private sector. I'm not sure whether a clipper chip will slow the crooks down, but I am convinced that anything anyone has conceived of in government can be recreated by someone in the private sector, and that attempts to prevent the dissemination of information, like encryption techniques, are a waste of time and energy unless all nations agree in an enforceable, verifiable way to live by the same standard. I am also confident that if our legal system is to continue to function, governments, as well as individuals and businesses that have suffered civil wrongs, need to be able to have access to otherwise private communications under agreed rules and limited conditions. The alternative is impunity for criminals with the resources to make their financial activities secret, and therefore their business arrangements beyond the reach of the law. If we want to avoid a cyberanarchy, we need a cyberorder to emerge, and emerge quickly. On this, as on so many other standards in a globalized world, governments and businesses need to come together and reach consensus on common standards and procedures.

This move will be resisted by the American Civil Liberties Union as well as by the National Rifle Association. We have seen a preview of this resistance in the U.S. debate during the summer of 1996 over chemical taggants. Taggants are bits of colored plastic, less than five hundredths of an inch long, that can be placed by manufacturers in explosives to identify them, like fingerprints. Every law-enforcement agency in the world believes that taggants would be an effective way to deter terrorism, through providing an essentially perfect road map to the purchaser. Invented by a Wisconsin professor in response to a wave of left-wing campus bombings in the 1970s, taggants led in their first year to the conviction of a man who responded to an adulterous affair by murdering his wife's lover with a truck bomb. Taggants are already required by law in Switzerland. But in the United States, opposition from the NRA has stopped their use for almost two decades. Those in Congress who oppose taggants actually have forbidden the U.S. government to even study them for over fourteen years.

In August 1996, when I tried to insist that our government mandate the introduction of these tiny plastic IDs in all explosives everywhere, other senators, recipients of campaign contributions from the NRA, blocked the effort. They argued that as a matter of civil liberties and constitutional freedoms, people should be free to use explosives without the government being able to trace them. Privately, some Republican senators claimed that they feared this legislation would create a "radical response" by some of the right-wing militias, and might even provoke more bombings. The notion that we should have our ability to deter or detect terrorist actions thus blocked by the threats of such attacks is one the United States should firmly reject. Unfortunately, this notion continues to block action in the U.S. Congress.

The government does not have the interest, time, or right to examine the debris of an explosive used for a proper purpose, such as demolishing an old building to make way for new construction. But law enforcement must be able to trace an explosion that has killed people back to the terrorists responsible.

Similarly, when computers are used criminally, law enforcement needs to be able to trace computer transactions back to the abuser. At the same time, the government needs to secure its computers so they cannot be violated at will by anyone with mischief in mind.

The computer systems that operate our telephone communications, financial operations, utilities, and airports must be rendered impervious to the incursions of criminals or terrorist hackers.

Had I written this book even four years ago, my warnings about crime and terrorism might have been dismissed as a jeremiad. Unfortunately, the bombings of the World Trade Center, the federal building in Oklahoma City, and the complex in Dhahran have provided me with examples I wish I did not have so readily at hand.

The damage done by international crime is rarely as specific and dramatic as that of a terrorist attack, but in fact it is greater. We cannot see with our own eyes the billions of dollars hemorrhaging out of our economy. We cannot directly feel the violation of our sovereignty and territorial integrity by the smugglers of narcotics and human beings. We cannot easily envision the harm to our national security through the failure of countries that once bravely struggled for the dignity of freedom. But we do hear the grieving of mothers on the evening news—whether their children are the victims of crime or the perpetrators, either way, it breaks hearts and ruins lives.

If, however, our intellect and imagination prove unable to connect the drive-by shooting with the jungle laboratory and the numbered account, to draw a line between the theft of our computer identity and transnational organizations whose interests and actions are diametrically opposed to those of civilized society, we will simply fail to understand the world we live in. Worse, we will fail to pass the torch at a critical junction in human history.

Just as it is abundantly clear that America cannot go it alone against global crime and terrorism, it is equally obvious that only America has the power and prestige to champion that cause, forge the alliances, lead the crusade.

We've done it twice before—in World War II and in the fifty-year struggle against communism. And we must do it a third time, and for the same reasons as before, so that those who would impose their will through deception and violence are vanquished and defanged.

Democracies are notoriously slow to rouse. But once roused, their ability to cooperate with one another, to unify their will, intelligence, and resources, can never be rivaled by that of their enemies, whether political or criminal, for their enemies' alliances are always founded on fear, compulsion, and temporary advantage. But the war we are fighting now is unlike wars of the past. Nondemocracies must join with us in this effort.

The most serious task of all, however, remains ours alone. The reason is clear. The greatest deficit in our fight against crime is *our* demand for drugs. Almost 70 percent of all our crime is drug related. Put simply: We are not losing the war on drugs— we have yet to fight a war!

Our failure to summon the will and resources to provide drug treatment on demand, drug education and health care to all our children, schools that stay open with after-hours programs for parents and students, adequate resources for law enforcement, and, most critically, the earliest interventions for children aged zero to three guarantees continued crisis at home and with our friends abroad. Addressing these concerns will enable us to make peace in our own country and contribute to it elsewhere.

The twenty-first century, which is already very much upon us, can, should, and must be a shining era in the life of man. An era of creativity, prosperity, and longevity. A century without the great wars that have stained all the centuries before. A renaissance in which, liberated from traditional boundaries of space and time, as well as drudgery, people will attain new levels of wealth, knowledge, and well-being.

Until we ensure that victory and enact that vision, we must never forget that what is at stake here is nothing less than the fate of civilization.

Will our lives be ones of peace and order, harmony and dignity? Or will we, our children, and their children pass their days in a dingy, dangerous world of venality and violence, a low-grade fever of criminality and corruption? Or, worse yet, will we slide into "global ungovernability," what the poet William Butler Yeats called "mere anarchy"? For that, he said, it was enough for the best to lack all conviction.

Those words must never describe us, the men and women living now, who by the force of history itself have been granted the task, challenge, and responsibility of defeating all those who would gladly sell a world of law and liberty for the riches of hell.

Notes

1: Darkness Visible

20 "The American century . . . ": Rosabeth Moss Kanter, *World Class: Thriving Locally in the Global Economy* (New York: Simon & Schuster, 1995), p. 22.

31 . . . we are dealing . . . : Bill Olson, statement to U.S. Senate Subcommittee on Terrorism, Narcotics and International Operations, *Hearings on Recent Developments in Transnational Crime Affecting U.S. Law Enforcement and Foreign Policy* (hereafter, *Hearings*), April 21, 1994.

2: Hijacking the Russian Bear

40 "Corruption is devouring . . . ": Yeltsin quoted in Claire Sterling, "Redfellas," *The New Republic*, April 11, 1994, p. 19.

41 " . . . if you make our economy . . . ": Kalugin quoted in Lev Timofeyev, *Russia's Secret Rulers: How the Government and Criminal Mafia Exercise Their Power* (New York: Knopf, 1992), p. 111.

42 . . . the smuggling trade . . . : Stephen Handelman, "The Russian 'Mafiya,' " *Foreign Affairs*, March/April 1994, pp. 87–88.

42 "These two fellows . . . ": quoted in "Mobs Prey on Soviet Entrepreneurs' Success," *Chicago Tribune*, October 14, 1991.

43 "A big proportion . . . ": quoted in "Many Russian Banks Linked to Mafia," Reuters, March 2, 1994.

43 "We know that . . . ": ibid.

44 "on the spot execution . . . ": quoted in Graham Frazer and George Lancelle, *Absolute Zhirinovsky* (New York: Penguin, 1994), pp. 102, 117.

46 "The Russian mafiya's . . . ": Handelman, "Russian 'Mafiya,' " p. 90.

48 "It's wonderful that . . . ": quoted in Sterling, "Redfellas," p. 22.

50 "Russia attracts . . . ": *Murmanskiy Vestnik*, March 19, 1996, in Foreign Broadcast Information Service 96-017-L.

3: CHINA ON THE BRINK

54 "In the 1980s . . . " quoted in Anthony Davis, "A Goldrush to Mayhem," *Asiaweek*, August 25, 1995.

59 "In the new world . . . ": William Kleinknecht, *The New Ethnic Mobs: The Changing Face of Organized Crime in America* (New York: Free Press, 1996), p. 92.

64 "The Colombian cartels . . . ": Roger Faligot, *The Invisible Empire: The Overseas Chinese* (New York: Putnam, 1995).

66 "All five of us . . . ": quoted in "A Grim Harvest in China's Prisons: Kidneys Removed After Executions," *Open Magazine*, January 1995.

66 "Everything is approved . . . ": ibid.

67 "I was ordered . . . ": quoted in " 'Confessions' by Activist Harry Wu," *Christian Science Monitor*, August 9, 1995.

4: WHO STOLE COLOMBIA?

70 ". . . as to whether . . . ": John J. Coleman, *Hearings*, April 21, 1994.

73 "the only thing . . . " Gabriel Taboada's testimony, *Hearings*, April 20, 1994.

73 "to such an extent . . . ": ibid.

75 Would the Government . . . : ibid.

79 The Colombian entry . . . : Paul F. Reid, "The Threat of Colombian Heroin," paper presented to *Hearings*.

81 " . . . an extensive investigation . . . ": Coleman, *Hearings*.

82 "arrest or surrender . . . ": *International Narcotics Control Strategy Report*, p. 81.

83 Columbian president Samper asked: "Motes, Beams and Drugs," *The Economist*, March 9, 1996, p. 18.

85 "We Deserve Him": *El Tiempo*, March 31, 1996, p. 4a.

5: Reengineering the Drug Trade

89 "People do whatever . . . ": quoted in Jeffrey Goldberg, "The Mafia's Morality Crisis," *New York* magazine, January 9, 1995, p. 26.

90 The Mafia has failed . . . : Peter Reuter and David Ronfeldt, "The Decline of the American Mafia," *Trends in Organized Crime,* vol. 1, no. 3 (Spring 1996), p. 27.

94 "Casso will tell . . . ": Selwyn Raab, "Former Lucchese Crime Boss Is to Testify on Russian Mob," *New York Times,* May 15, 1996.

94 The combination . . . : Paul Stares, *Global Habit: The Drug Problem in a Borderless World* (Washington, DC: Brookings Institution, in press), ms. pp. 39–40 of ch. 2.

96 ". . . if you compare . . . ": Lagos NTA television network, 2000 GMT, April 13, 1996, transcribed and printed by the Foreign Broadcast Information Service in *Narcotics,* April 16, 1996, p. 54.

96 "Drug control . . . ": Stares, *Global Habit,* ms. p. 29 of ch. 2.

102 "the Mexican drug problem . . . ": Paul Reuter and David Ronfeldt, "Quest for Integrity: The Mexican-U.S. Drug Issue in the 1980s," Rand Note N-3266-USDP (Santa Monica, CA: Rand Corporation, 1991).

106 "One day . . . ": quoted in Barry Collins, "The Seeds of Misery," *The Times* of London, November 14, 1993.

106 "marketing miracle . . . ": ibid.

108 If previous experience . . . : Stares, *Global Habit,* ms. p. 22 of ch. 4.

6: The Globalization of Terror

111 "the deliberate . . . ": Benjamin Netanyahu, "Defining Terrorism," in Netanyahu, ed., *Terrorism: How the West Can Win* (New York: Farrar, Straus and Giroux, 1986), p. 9.

112 "What has the PLO . . . ": Paul Johnson, "The Cancer of Terrorism," in Netanyahu, *Terrorism,* p. 35.

115 "A rusty freighter . . . ": Malcolm Gray and William Lowther, "The 'Loose Nukes,' " *Maclean's,* April 22, 1996, p. 24.

115 "In the not-so-distant . . . ": Todd Crowell, "The End of the Cold War Has Made Nuclear Terror More Likely," *Asiaweek,* October 6, 1995, p. 50.

116 "a major . . . ": quoted in Gray and Lowther, " 'Loose Nukes,' " p. 25.

117 "If wrapped . . . ": Marvin Cetron quoted in James Kitfield, "The Age of Superterrorism," *National Journal Government Executive,* July 1995.

118 Do you have . . . : Dzhokhar Dudayev interviewed by Yuri Zarakhovich, *Time,* March 4, 1996, p. 43.

120 "When you talk . . . ": *National Journal Government Executive*, July 1995.

122 "The Industrial Revolution . . . ": quoted in John Douglas and Mark Olshaker, *Unabomber: On the Trail of America's Most Wanted Serial Killer* (New York: Pocket, 1996), p. 191.

125 "When the common criminal . . . ": André Bacard, "*Playboy* Interview," *Playboy*, February 1996.

127 "create significant . . . ": Department of Defense *Awareness Document* quoted in Keith Stone, "Cyberspace Crawls with Crooks, Spies, Computer Cops Warn," *Houston Chronicle*, September 11, 1994.

127 *Information Warfare:* Sue Nelson, *Information Warfare for Dummies: A Guide for the Perplexed*, March 5, 1996, unpaged.

129 The high-energy pulse . . . : ibid.

132 "Trusting the government . . . ": quoted in "Privacy for Sale in the Age of Information," *Arizona Republic*, February 15, 1996.

132 "There has to . . . ": quoted in "Arguments Reached on Encryption Rules," *Euromoney*, February 1996.

7: Human Contraband

133 "It is a fundamental . . . ": Memorandum for the Heads of Executive Departments and Agencies, February 7, 1995.

137 At the time . . . : William Kleinknecht, *The New Ethnic Mobs: The Changing Face of Organized Crime in America* (New York: Free Press, 1996), p. 163.

138 "PRC alien smugglers . . . ": Executive Intelligence Brief: *Potential Areas of Concern for the U.S. Immigration and Naturalization Service.* U.S. Department of Justice, HQ-EB-95-1, p. 4.

141 "trained assassins . . . ": ibid., p. 6.

144 ". . . between April and October 1980 . . . ": Alex Schmid and Ernesto Savona, "Migration and Crime: A Framework for Discussion," *Trends in Organized Crime*, vol. 1, no. 3 (Spring 1996), p. 79.

147 "Russian Customs officials . . . ": U.S. Department of Justice, Strategic Assessment: *The Use of Moscow by Transit Migrants to Access the West*, December 28, 1994, p. 14.

8: Where the Dirty Money Washes Up

153 There are four . . . : Jeffrey Robinson, *The Laundrymen* (New York: Arcade, 1996), p. 10. (Quoted from galleys.)

159 Use of the UBS . . . : Drug Enforcement Administration Intelligence Division report *Asian Money Movement Methods*, DEA-

94023, prepared by the Financial Unit of the Strategic Intelligence Section, p. 12.

160 "... money laundering haven ... ": U.S. Department of State, *International Narcotics*, March 1996, p. 565.

161 Salinas verse: *New York Times*, June 5, 1996, p. A12.

161 Loutchansky: S.C. Gwynne and Larry Gurwin, "The Russia Connection," *Time*, July 8, 1996, pp. 32–36.

164 "What do we ... ": quoted in Robert I. Friedman, "The Money Plane," *New York* magazine, January 22, 1996, p. 27.

164 "That's my responsibility ... ": ibid.

164 "If you rip ... ": ibid., p. 26.

9: A VISION OF VICTORY

173 The movie *Bonnie and Clyde* ... : *Hearings*, April 21, 1994.

174 ... trafficking groups ... : Stares, *Global Habit*, ms. pp. 27–28 of ch. 4.

178 "... it is not unthinkable ... ": Supreme Court Associate Justice John Paul Stevens quoted by Mireya Navarro in "When Drug Kingpins Fall, Illicit Assets Buy a Cushion," *New York Times*, March 19, 1996, p. A20.

184 If the FBI ... : Louis J. Freeh, *The FBI's Presence Overseas*, pp. iii–iv.

185 "*not* intelligence officers ... ": ibid., p. v.

Index